UPROOTED!

Refugees and Forced Migrants

Elizabeth G. Ferris

Friendship Press • New York

Copyright © 1998 by Friendship Press

Editorial Offices:
475 Riverside Drive, New York, NY 10115-0050

Distribution Office:
P.O. Box 37844, Cincinnati, OH 45222-0844

Scripture quotations are from the New Revised Standard Version of the
Bible, copyright 1989 by the Division of Christian Education of the
National Council of the Churches of Christ in the USA. Used by per-
mission. All rights reserved.

Manufactured in the United States of America

Library of Congress Cataloging-in-Publication Data

Ferris, Elizabeth G.
    Uprooted! : refugees and forced migrants / Elizabeth G. Ferris.
        p.   cm.
    Includes bibliographical references.
    ISBN 0-377-00319-0
    1. Refugees. 2. Refugees—Government policy—Religious aspects.
3. Emigration and immigration—Religious aspects—Christianity.
4. International relief.   I. Title.
    HV640.F433   1998
    362.87—dc21   97-18121
                                                          CIP

To my wonderful family—Barry, Jon, and Sara—who provide the support and love that makes it possible for me to work and write and still have a life

Contents

INTRODUCTION vii

ONE 1

Fifty Million Uprooted
    Words That Make a Difference
    Traditional Solutions

TWO 19

Why They Flee
    Economic Causes
    Environmental Causes
    Political Factors
    Ethnic Conflicts
    War
    Civilian Casualties of War
    Economic Consequences of War

THREE 33

Rwanda, Center of a Maelstrom
    A Troubled Past
    The War Begins
    A Plane Crash—and Genocide
    The UN Acts
    The Tragedy of Goma
    The Repatriation Dilemma
    Lessons from Rwanda

FOUR 69

Two Nations of Immigrants
    Nations of Immigrants
    Refugee Resettlement
        Canada
        United States
    Responding to Strangers on the Border
        Canada
        United States
    Challenges to Current U.S. and Canadian Policy
        Canada and Human Rights Instruments
        The United States and Immigration Legislation
    Advocacy

FIVE 97

Becoming the Church of the Stranger
    Starting with a Story
    Taking the First Step
    Addressing the Causes

APPENDIX: TABLES OF STATISTICS 109

NOTES 113

FOR FURTHER READING 115

VIDEOGRAPHY 117

PHOTO ESSAY 55

Introduction

Approximately ten years ago, I visited ecumenical refugee workers in eastern Sudan who were working with the victims of the horrifying Ethiopian famine of 1985. As we toured the camps and feeding centers where the ravages of starvation were all too evident, and saw the conditions in which the ecumenical refugee ministry was being carried out, I felt an overwhelming sense of humility. The conditions in which we in the United States work are so different—so much easier.

On that trip I met an American nurse and said, "How do you stand it here? With 130 degree heat, no running water, no electrity, poverty and isolation all around you—how do you keep going?" The nurse laughed and said, "This is a million times easier than working on policy in the United States." Seeing my puzzled look, she went on to explain. "Physical conditions may be bad here, but every day I see the positive results of my work. I see children getting stronger because of the work I do. I see people beginning to rebuild their lives. Believe me, it's much harder to try influencing U.S. policy."

Although I don't remember the nurse's name, her words have stayed with me over the years. Christians in all parts of the world are working in very different contexts to minister to the uprooted people among them. Our responsibility in the United States and Canada is the same as it is for Christians in Sudan or Lebanon or Thailand: being faithful to the gospel mandate of working for justice and reaching out to those who come to us as strangers.

ONE

Fifty Million Uprooted

My mother sent me to the market to buy some food. When I came back, I saw the house was in flames. My mother, father, and sister were all killed. A missile had hit our house. Everyone was running away, the rebels were getting closer and closer—killing everyone in their way. I saw the bodies of my family and the bodies of my neighbors. I didn't know what to do—so I started running, too. I was fourteen then. That was six years ago—the war in Liberia is still going on. I'm still a refugee in Sierra Leone. I wonder if I'll ever be able to go home.

—Saul Joseph, Liberian refugee in Sierra Leone. From an interview with the author, June 1996.

This is a book about people who are forced to leave their homes, their communities, their countries. It is not about people who take a job in another land because travel is broadening, or people who migrate because they want a better life for their children.

This is a book about people who are *forced* to leave their communities because otherwise they would die. Some leave because of war. Some are forced to flee in the middle of the night because they have been singled out for persecution. Some go because of famine or economic exploitation. The reasons are many, but what these people all have in common is that they leave their countries because of fear.

Forced migration is an old story. Since biblical times, people have been forced to flee their homes because of hunger, war, and oppression. One of the central themes of the Old Testament is that of a people in exile, and the Hebrew texts are filled with admonitions to welcome the stranger. It has been said that the Bible is the ultimate immigration handbook, written by, for, and about immigrants and refugees. It begins with Adam and Eve, exiled from the Garden of Eden to make their home in a new land (Gen. 1). Noah and his family were victims of a natural disaster, making it necessary for them to rebuild their world (Gen. 6–10). Abraham and Sarah were sent from their land to a place to which God led them (Gen. 12:1–3). Moses—a criminal alien fleeing for his life—returned to the promised land in search of religious freedom. God accompanied the people on their way to exile (2 Kings 24:10ff; 2 Chron. 36:15–23), protected them (Esther, David), and finally brought them back after fifty years. Ruth followed her mother-in-law back to Judah, and was dependent on Boaz for food and life (Ruth). The Old Testament prophets fled for their lives, found protection, and were held in strange lands (Exod. 1; Deut. 10:17–19). Popular backlash against immigrants and political scapegoating of foreigners is a theme that runs through Ezra and Nehemiah.

> **You shall not deprive a resident alien or an orphan of justice; you shall not take a widow's garment in pledge. Deut. 24:17.**

In the New Testament, the Messiah became an undocumented refugee fleeing to Egypt with his parents, Mary and Joseph, to escape political persecution and death (Matt. 2:13ff).

> **Now after they had left, an angel of the Lord appeared to Joseph in a dream and said, "Get up, take the child and his mother, and flee to Egypt, and remain there until I tell you; for Herod is about to search for the child, to destroy him." Matt. 2:13–14.**

Jesus lived out his life as an itinerant preacher with no place to lay his head (Matt. 8:20; 13:54–57). Throughout the New Testament, strangers are affirmed and included as those for whom Christ died.

There is no longer Jew or Greek, there is no longer slave or free, there is no longer male and female; for all of you are one in Christ Jesus. Gal. 3:28.

For centuries, churches and individual Christians have welcomed strangers—long before governmental policies were developed or United Nations agencies created. Throughout the Middle Ages, monasteries offered rest for travelers and strangers. Widows and deaconesses, in particular, practiced hospitality (1 Tim. 5:10). Many women—later elevated to sainthood—dedicated their lives to the homeless and uprooted in their midst. St. Anysia in Thessalonica (third century), Olympias the Deaconness in Constantinople (fourth century), and Julietta the Merciful in Russia (sixteenth century) are only three of the most notable examples. Churches were sanctuaries for those fleeing persecution, violence, and vengeance. Churches provided a home and a welcome for immigrants arriving in North American cities at the turn of the century. Christians were in the forefront of desperate efforts to smuggle Jews out of Nazi Germany. Indeed, it was cooperation among the churches during World War II—to get people out of Germany after the war, and, later, to respond to the needs of millions of displaced Europeans—that led to the formation of the World Council of Churches and the modern ecumenical movement.

North Americans have a long history of responding to strangers, of ministering to refugees, of welcoming the persecuted. It is a part of our Christian tradition. For Christians living in North America, it is also part of our national identity—our cultural heritage. However, we dare not romanticize that heritage. Many who came to these lands were forced migrants, and the slave traders and owners justified that practice with the same Bible we use. Others came to make their fortunes, to escape justice, because they saw an opportunity for a better life, or because they did not fit in back at home.

However, although Canada and the United States were havens for all kinds of people seeking safety and freedom for all sorts of reasons, those migrations were devastating for the original inhabitants of the continent—and for many of the migrants. The welcome extended to early explorers by aboriginal people was repaid with violence, displacement, and death. Furthermore, many of the migrants whose descendants now make up a substantial percentage of our population did not come willingly. Slaves were hunted in Africa by greedy traders—black and white—who bound them in chains and tossed them onto ships headed for the new world. For good or for bad, immigration has largely shaped our cultures and identities—in the case of native peoples, almost destroying theirs. Immigrants have created and developed our traditions and political institutions, our laws and our songs. Immigration made Canada and the United States into the nations they are today. Sometimes we forget that.

In our own day, people are being uprooted on an unprecedented scale. Scarcely a day goes by without a report of people being displaced. Genocide in Rwanda led a million people to cross into other countries during a single week in July 1994. A million people fleeing for their lives! In one sense, they were lucky. They survived the slaughter, and the borders were open. In June 1996, shiploads of desperate refugees from the carnage in Monrovia spent weeks traveling from port to port in West Africa. No one would allow them to land and the ships returned to Liberia.

The terrible reality is that no country wants refugees. As the world becomes a global village with a universal corporate culture and with communication systems that crisscross national borders, governments are competing with one another to find new ways of keeping refugees out. The same governments that open their borders to goods and capital, close them to the movement of people. The Canadian government is the only one in the world that requires refugees to pay a fee—$975—to be allowed entry, or "landing." The U.S. government has instructed its Coast Guard to intercept rickety boats of Haitians or Cubans and return the would-be refugees to their home countries.

Even as European governments formulate sophisticated means of integrating their economies, these procedures are accompanied by exclusion. Fortress Europe, Fortress America, Fortress Canada—the walls are going up. And, of course, it is not just the rich countries of the world that are trying to keep refugees out. The government of Kenya announced in the mid-1990s that it had had enough of Somali refugees—that they must all go home. In 1996, the government of Sierra Leone closed its borders to Liberian refugees, saying, "We have our own problems; we can't handle any more." Fifteen thousand Vietnamese who have been living in Hong Kong refugee camps for eight years are in the process of being sent back to Vietnam.

No country wants refugees, but we live in a time during which increasing numbers of people are being uprooted from their homes. Ours is an era of virulent wars and of international institutions that watch helplessly as countries degenerate into spasms of violence and bloodshed. Meanwhile, weapons of mass destruction—particularly landmines—displace millions of people and make it difficult for them to return home. And once the peace agreements are signed, the attention of the international community moves on. But peace is a fragile condition. It needs to be nurtured and requires sustained attention. In the fall of 1996, the German government announced that the 350,000 Bosnians who had sought refuge in Germany would have to return to Bosnia in six months. There is a peace agreement in Bosnia, the German government said, and the refugees can all go home.

But peace in Bosnia is fragile. Towns and villages have been "ethnically cleansed." How can a Bosnian Muslim go home when her town has been taken over by Serbs? When her house is now occupied by a Serb who, in turn, was displaced by fighting in his village? Who will protect the woman if she tries to reclaim her house? Who will decide on her right to occupy the house in that small village? What will be the impact on newly created Bosnian political institutions and a devastated economy of 3 million returning Bosnians who have been living in exile in other European countries or as internally displaced people? And how can Bosnians "return" to towns they never lived in?

When an alien resides with you in your land, you shall not oppress the alien. The alien who resides with you shall be to you as the citizen among you; you shall love the alien as yourself, for you were aliens in the land of Egypt: I am the Lord your God. Lev. 19:33–34.

The issues are complex, the numbers overwhelming. Today there are 50 million uprooted people in the world—on every continent. But behind the statistics and numbers, beyond the complexities of political analysis, are individual human beings—children of God.

> I lost my home, my community . . . everything . . . . My husband stayed behind . . . my six-year-old child was too sick to come with us so they took her to another camp . . . .I don't know where is my eleven-year-old son . . . . I worry about my husband, my children who are not with me, my daughter and my son, my relatives . . . . Will life ever be normal again? Will our family ever be together again? I am grateful to be away from the killing but don't feel safe . . . . Many women in this camp were raped when they fled and even in the camp it is not safe. Who can I ask for help? Will they understand me? Who can I trust? Will peace come to our people?
>
> —Rwandan refugee woman. *A Moment to Choose: Risking to Be with Uprooted People, A Resource Book.* Geneva: World Council of Churches, 1997.

This book consists of five chapters. We begin with a survey of the present situation of uprooted people and then look at the underlying reasons for displacement. Why are so many people forced to leave their homes? Because a discussion of root causes can be abstract, we then look at one concrete example—Rwanda—to see the interrelationships among the various forces that lead to the uprooting of people, and to examine the reasons that make it so difficult to fix a situation. Then we come back to North America and look at what is happening in the United States and Canada. Finally, we open ourselves to the challenge of the gospel message: What does it mean to welcome strangers in today's world?

Words That Make a Difference

Even though people who are forced to leave their communities share a common sense of homelessness, they are labeled and treated differently, depending on the reasons for their flight, the course of their journey, and who is making the distinction.

A Glossary of Terms

Refugees are defined by international law as persons who have fled persecution because of race, religion, nationality, opinion, or membership in a particular social group, and who are unable or, out of fear, "unwilling to avail [themselves] of the protection of that country" and are outside their country of origin.—1951 UN Convention and 1967 Protocol on the Status of Refugees.

Asylum-seekers (or in Canada **refugee claimants**) are people who arrive by land, sea, or air in a particular country and claim refugee status based on the above definition of refugees.

Internally displaced persons are those "who have been forced to flee their homes suddenly or unexpectedly in large numbers as a result of armed conflict, internal strife, systematic violations of human rights, or natural or man-made disasters; and who are within the territory of their own country."—UN Economic and Social Council, "Analytical Report of the Secretary-General on Internally Displaced Persons," Geneva, 1992.

International migrants are people who move to another country to live or work temporarily, and those who emigrate, eventually to settle permanently. Some international migrants leave their countries voluntarily, but some are forced to leave because they cannot survive at home. Most international migrants come with the permission of the host country, but growing numbers are considered undocumented, or illegal. That is, they bypass normal immigration channels to enter a country.

Governments take these distinctions very seriously. Under international conventions, they are required to treat refugees differently from migrants who come for economic reasons. According to international law, governments have the right to determine who will be considered a refugee. Even though there are international standards that specify the criteria for determining refugee status, it is governments which make that determination. Both the United States and Canadian governments have complex procedures for hearing the person's case and deciding whether or not he or she is, in fact, a refugee. Political considerations enter into the process as well. Thus, the United States government refused to acknowledge that Salvadorans and Guatemalans fleeing violence in their countries in the 1980s were refugees. In part, this refusal was because the United States government was supporting the governments of those countries, and to recognize victims of violence caused by those governments would undermine U.S. policies in the region.

Even more dramatic was the very different treatment accorded Cubans and Haitians arriving on Florida's shores in the early 1990s. Until 2 May 1995, Cubans arriving by boat were allowed to resettle in the United States and become citizens if they chose to do so. Haitians, on the other hand, were intercepted by the U.S. Coast Guard and returned to Haiti. The Castro government was an enemy of the United States; it was thus politically important to recognize people fleeing that regime as refugees. But, even though there was serious persecution in Haiti under the Duvalier regime, and a military coup in 1990, the U.S. government refused to allow more than a handful of Haitians to enter its territory as refugees. Cubans and Haitians were not treated alike because the U.S. government had different policies toward their respective governments. And, as many observers have pointed out, race was undoubtedly a factor. The difference in United States policies toward Haitians and Cubans came to an end in May 1995, when the government announced that henceforth Cubans and Haitians would be treated alike: they would all be returned to their home countries.

In practice, governments use different criteria at different times to determine who is a refugee. In 1993, a ship named the *Golden Venture* ran aground in New York harbor and three hundred Chinese were apprehended for illegal entry into the United States. A few of the Chinese were found to be refugees, most were eventually deported, but all of them remained in detention for as long as three years. As the following story shows, people left China because they were afraid, but it was hard to prove that they had been singled out for persecution because of a reason specified in the definition of refugees. Most of the Chinese who fled claimed they had left China because of its policy of limiting families to one child. The U.S. government claimed that this policy affected most Chinese. Therefore, these individuals were not singled out for persecution and thus were not eligible for refugee status. Moreover, there was a fear that if the men on the *Golden*

Venture were accepted as refugees on this basis, many more Chinese would seek to come to the United States.

Today I live a life facing the iron bars of prison. Like all other Chinese of my age, I was caught in the family planning conflict. We are allowed one child. If our first child is a girl, we can try for a second child—the son we need to guarantee our care in our old age. My wife and I have two daughters. In our yearning for a son, she became pregnant again. The family planning people found out and, when she was in her ninth month of pregnancy, came to our home to force her to have an abortion. She was not there, and so they took me for forced sterilization.

I was terrified. I had seen what happened to other members of my family who were sterilized. We do not have the technology that you do. Once sterilized, we are no longer able to work the farms. Our ability to support our families is gone. We become social outcasts—we are seen as eunuchs—we have lost our place in society. Our life becomes one of being among the living dead.

My fear was overwhelming. They put me on a truck to transport me to a sterilization site. In terror, I jumped from the moving vehicle. When I fell, I broke all my teeth. A member of the family planning team saw me and jumped after me. He was hit by a car, and I was blamed. I was beaten and imprisoned in a makeshift jail in my village. I was fined the equivalent of five years' earnings. My family could not pay. My house was ransacked and all my family's belongings were taken. My family fled—they arrested my father and imprisoned and beat him. He committed suicide while in prison. Eventually my wife was caught and our child forcibly aborted, just days before he would have been born.

While in jail, I saw an opportunity and escaped. My hope was to reach the United States, work off my passage, and then save every penny I could to help my family. There was no chance to do this in China. If I were found, I would be imprisoned, beaten and possibly killed. I had brought shame on the government when my father committed suicide . . . .

You, the people of America, are my only hope. In this country I have learned about God. China is a Godless country. In this country, I have learned about the love of Jesus Christ. In this country, I pray I will find my freedom.

—From "In Search of a Better Hell," a dramatic monologue by Joan M. Maruskin, 1994.

In situations of widespread violence, such as Rwanda or Bosnia, people fleeing generalized violence are treated as refugees without individual refugee determination processes.

Although refugees are defined as those who have crossed an international border because of persecution or war, far larger numbers of people have fled their communities for the same reasons but have remained within their countries of origin. Latin America, for example, produces relatively few refugees, but there are as many as 3 million internally displaced people—particularly in Peru and Colombia. Internally displaced people are usually far more vulnerable to violence since they are closer to the conflict that displaced them and to the enemies who continue to pursue them.

When I was 14, guerrillas came to my village in the Peruvian Andes. It was 1981, and they were unarmed. They said they came to teach us and punish those who exploited the village, like thieves and corrupt landowners. They promised to build roads and health clinics (which to this day do not exist).

Instead they began to kill. At first, it was only those who opposed them. But after the military arrived, and themselves began to commit abuses, the guerrillas killed people who they believed were helping the soldiers. My grandfather, who had given an army patrol water, was among those they killed. Although we wept and pleaded for his life, the guerrillas [tortured him until he died].

The soldiers would ask us to feed them. If we refused, they called us *terrucos*, Quechua for "terrorist." Yet, if we fed the soldiers, the guerrillas said we were traitors. One night, soldiers came for my father. The next morning, we found his mutilated body with a sign that read "All the *terrucos* will die this way."

That is where our great sadness began. We ate only tears. Later, guerrillas seized my brother; I never saw him again. In 1983, we fled our village in the middle of the night with several other families. We became *desplazados* [the displaced].

Although we did not realize it until much later, we were part of a huge exodus. Thousands of families were forced to abandon their homes, lands, and animals. I carried my grandmother, who could not walk, on my back. Once, we had to hide in a cactus patch to elude the guerrillas, who would have killed us. My nieces and nephews fainted with hunger and exhaustion as we scaled the mountains, with only the blankets we had managed to grab, for shelter.

In the city, we found not safety but suspicion. People glared at us and called us terrorists. Fearful, we could not say we were *desplazados*. Hired to work the fields, we were fed only once a day. When we arrived in Huancayo, we slept for days in the street, until a woman took pity on us and sent us to a family with spare rooms. We cleaned their house in exchange for rent, but often went for days without eating. . . .

Slowly, we began to rebuild our lives. I joined an association of displaced persons and began to teach others about their rights. For money, I washed clothes, cleaned houses, and did some weaving. Today, we still eat just twice a day, and around me I see our children suffering from malnutrition and disease, especially tuberculosis. . . .

We do not want to end our lives as *desplazados*. But neither are we willing to remain in the shadows, forgotten victims of a war most Peruvians are anxious to forget. If there is to be peace in Peru, our children will be the ones to build it. Born in flight, they hold the seeds for renewal. For them, we demand more.

—Isabel Suasnabur Huarocc. From "We Ate Only Tears," *World Refugee Survey, 1995,* pp. 184–85. Washington, DC: U.S. Committee for Refugees.

Providing assistance for internally displaced people is usually more difficult than providing aid for refugees because the ongoing violence in an area creates logistical and political problems for relief agencies: roads may be impassable, relief convoys may be subject to attack, and warring parties may view such activities with suspicion. Thus, in Sri Lanka internally displaced people are subjected to bombings and the continuing clashes between insurgent groups and the government. And the difficulties of both protection and assistance for the internally displaced in Sudan, Peru, and Liberia are far greater than for refugees from those same countries who are living in neighboring countries. Frequently, internally displaced people do not wish to be identified because they are afraid of drawing attention to themselves.

While refugees have access to an international system of protection and assistance (although that system is often inadequate), there is no mechanism for response to the needs of internally displaced people.

Today the displaced are seen as more alien to the Sudanese than we Eritreans. The concern about the presence of strangers has shifted to the southerners.

As a refugee, I understand many of their concerns and fears. They have passed through the same traumas as we. In a way the displaced are crossing a border coming from the south to the north. The north is alien for them. The environment, weather, language, religion, customs, traditions—all are unfamiliar, all are barriers to their being welcome in the north.

The vast majority of them do not speak Arabic, and most of them are farmers, not urban dwellers. Many from the villages have never seen a car or a tarmac road. Some get killed simply because they do not know how to walk around in town . . . .

The feeling of living a temporary existence has a detrimental effect on the structure of the family. No one sinks roots. Every shelter has a transient air, as though those who live within will depart momentarily. Yet this temporariness can last for years and years.

The displaced enter into illegal means for making money by brewing beer, gambling, hustling illegal goods, or working as prostitutes just to make ends meet. They go through much degradation. At home they are independent; they have a patch of land and some animals. Here they have nothing . . . .

It is very depressing to make visits to the slum areas where they have built their shanty towns. As many as fifteen people live in an area no larger than 4 by 4 meters [13 by 13 feet]. When we made our health survey in one of the fringe camps, most of the children were malnourished. Many of them weighed 85 percent or less of weight for height . . . . Whatever the displaced earn in wages, it seems they can't give their families more than one substantial meal a day. Many cannot even give that.

Those of us who are refugees know we are in bad shape. Yet for the displaced it is worse. The fact that they are Sudanese hinders them from getting special care from the United Nations or international organizations. No one can plead their case. Those relief agencies who have some access to the displaced find that it is really beyond their capacity to do anything that will really make a difference for them. No help we give shows any remarkable effects. They need more help than any relief agencies can give.

—Tesega, Eritrean refugee and relief worker. From *Disposable People?: The Plight of Refugees* by Judy Mayotte, pp. 266–67. New York: Orbis Books, 1992.

Although matters of definition are important, they sometimes get in the way of efficient response to people in need. Increasingly, churches use the term *uprooted* for all who are forced to leave their homes, be they refugees, economic migrants, or internally displaced persons. The uprooted are those who have been forced to flee because of violence, persecution, or starvation, and include people who have crossed a national border as well as those who are internally displaced. The term *uprooted* evokes the image of a tree pulled from the ground—just as people are pulled up by their roots from their communities.

Traditional solutions

Traditionally three long-term, or "durable," solutions are advocated for refugees. *Voluntary repatriation*—going home—remains the best. But as wars last longer, voluntary repatriation becomes less likely for many of the world's refugees. Moreover, as countries accommodating large numbers of refugees try to ease their own burdens, they may encourage or coerce refugees to return before conditions are safe. Finally, refugees often return to communities that have been devastated by the very violence that drove them out. In the early 1980s, Central Americans were deported from the United States back to situations of conflict—even though they expressed fear about what would happen to them. In 1997, Bosnians were being returned from Europe—even though their villages were occupied by the people who had forced them to flee in the first place.

So many of us were so eager to return to our homes, but it was not as simple as we had supposed. . . . After we learned about the dreadful condition of our village, we decided we had better remain in Teseney for a while. Those of us who were refugees went to the edge of the village to build whatever shelter we could. I saw that some who had been there six months or more built round shelters of mud and stone, the sort we lived in before the war. My sons don't know how to build that sort of structure, and I am not sure I remember. It has been so many years. . . .

There is little left of Teseney's hospital. By the time we arrived, we were told that only one physician, four nurses, one midwife, and fifteen health assistants served a population of 60,000 to 70,000 people. . . .

> Food in Teseney is as scarce as it is in the rest of the country. Almost the whole country depends on relief assistance. The drought is very bad right now, and with the war just over, we have very few resources to try to feed ourselves.
>
> —Medhanie, returning Eritrean refugee. From *Disposable People?: The Plight of Refugees* by Judy Mayotte, pp. 287–88. New York: Orbis Books, 1992.

Local integration into the country of asylum is a second solution for refugees, and many have been welcomed into their host communities. But, as political and economic conditions in the countries of asylum deteriorate, governments may eventually adopt less welcoming policies. In countries, for example, where national unemployment rates approach 50 percent, governments are reluctant to welcome or allow refugees to stay because they are seen to compete with citizens for available jobs.

While the third solution, *resettlement to third countries*, has traditionally been used for a small percentage of the world's refugees, it has nonetheless been an important safety valve in some cases and a way of preserving first asylum in others. But today, traditional resettlement countries are reducing the number of refugees they will take and are making it more difficult for refugees from some countries to gain admittance. Canada and the United States have been world leaders in resettling refugees since World War II; but both countries, as we shall see in chapter 4, have cut refugee admissions by large percentages in the past several years.

The Office of the United Nations High Commissioner for Refugees (UNHCR) has been the focal point for protecting and assisting refugees. Since 1951 it has carried out its mandate with integrity and success, and has worked in close cooperation with the churches. But UNHCR is changing. Increasingly it has been asked to care for other categories of uprooted people. For example, its leadership role in assisting not only refugees but internally displaced people in the former Yugoslavia has fundamentally altered the agency.

In 1996, about half of UNHCR's budget was devoted to operations in former Yugoslavia. Yet of the world's 50 million or so uprooted people, "only" 3 million are in the former Yugoslavia. The issues involved in assisting displaced Bosnians are complex—

but complex emergencies are increasing, as is evident in the Central Asian republics of the former Soviet Union. The number of major humanitarian crises in which UNHCR is engaged has, by the agency's own admission, left it "stretched to the limit." Many of the issues facing UNHCR raise ethical questions: How do you respond to people in refugee camps when the camps are controlled by armed factions? Do you continue giving assistance to needy people when you know that some of it is being used to obtain weapons? When conditions in camps are very bad, do you encourage people to return home—even when the violence that caused them to flee continues? How strongly can Western governments be criticized when they are the agency's major donors?

Uprooted people have never had it easy. Each era has had its difficulties. But for a number of reasons, the situation facing uprooted people today is particularly hard:

1. Their numbers are increasing, and although there have been slightly fewer refugees in recent years, the number of internally displaced people is on the rise.

2. Although there are uprooted people on all continents, most of them remain in their regions of origin. Currently, some 93 percent of refugees and internally displaced people are located in countries of the South.

3. No one wants refugees. Governments of poor countries see them as a drain on their economies, a burden for their environments, and a complicating political factor. Some governments resist allowing refugees to enter, because they fear that the violence which drove the refugees out may spread to their own countries. Governments of rich countries fear that if refugees are allowed to cross their borders, they will serve as magnets for many more refugees. Popular backlash against foreigners is not just a Northern phenomenon—as the following quotation makes clear. It is a global reality.

As far as many are concerned, all foreigners are illegal immigrants. The press and media run stories suggesting that the country is being submerged by an endless tide of aliens, and accuses them of drug-trafficking, gun-running and other criminal activities. At a time when the country is experiencing a disturbing increase in vio-

4. The pressure to return refugees to their home countries has
   never been greater. Since early 1990, more than 3 million
   refugees have returned home as a result of massive and
   expensive operations in such countries as Cambodia, El
   Salvador, Namibia, Mozambique, and Nicaragua.

5. The issues are getting "messier." The gray area between economic and political motivation for flight is getting larger.
   People leave not only because they are afraid they will be
   killed in a war in their own country, but because that war has
   destroyed the economic infrastructure, making it impossible
   for them to sell their produce in the markets. They leave
   because the war has destroyed schools and clinics. It is getting harder and harder to distinguish between a refugee and
   an economic migrant from a country in conflict. Sometimes
   people leave because they anticipate future violence. Jewish
   refugees from the former Soviet Union, for example, often
   want to leave because of increasing signs of anti-Semitism
   and their fears that conditions will get much worse. Likewise,
   many African refugees have fled imminent violence. When
   there are signs that upheaval and persecution are increasing,
   persons will often leave without waiting to have violence or
   persecution visited upon them personally and directly.

6. The nature of warfare—particularly the deliberate displacement of people as a strategy of conflict—makes solutions
   more elusive. What will happen to Bosnian Muslims whose
   community is now in Serb territory? How can people return
   when those who tortured them and killed their relatives now
   constitute the police force?

7. The widespread use of landmines makes it particularly difficult for refugees to return. Even though peace agreements
   have been signed, landmines strewn during times of war continue to claim lives. In 1996 alone, an estimated 26,000 peo-

ple were killed or maimed because of landmines. How can people go home when their fields are littered with deadly explosives?

8. Although there is increasing talk of preventing wars and massive forced migration, there is, in fact, little political will to do so. The international community responds generously when a crisis erupts and is covered by the media. In the case of Rwanda, more than $2 billion in assistance was mobilized in April 1994 as 2 million refugees poured into neighboring countries during that year. Two billion is almost twice as much as UNHCR spends in one year on all of the world's refugees! But, despite the response to Rwandan refugees, violence is currently escalating in neighboring Burundi and the former Zaire, and most knowledgeable observers fear further bloodbaths. But the international community seems unable and unwilling to take effective action to prevent further escalation of the violence.

9. Moreover, the world has a short attention span. Two years after the crisis in Rwanda, UNHCR began closing clinics and schools in the refugee camps because of insufficient funds. The refugees were still there, the needs still monumental, but the world's attention had moved on to other crises. Insufficient funds increased pressure on the refugees to return home.

Most of the world's uprooted—whether they are called refugees, migrants, asylum-seekers, or internally displaced—are forced to leave their communities because of violence. But violence comes in many forms. In the next chapter we examine more closely some of the reasons for displacement. Why do people leave?

Two

Why They Flee

People are forced to leave their homes for many different reasons, but underlying them all is poverty or violence—frequently both. Although the times have changed, these are the same reasons why people fled their homes in biblical times. Joseph was able to bring his family out to Egypt when there was hunger in Israel. In fact, Joseph rose to power in Egypt because of his astute policy response to famine in the land. Naomi left the land of Judah with her husband and sons because of famine. When the three men died and conditions improved at home, she returned, bringing her foreign daughter-in-law with her.

As in Old Testament times, people today move back and forth. When conditions are bad, they leave their communities. When things improve, they often return home. The Israelites went to Egypt because of famine at home, but when political oppression in Egypt became unbearable they decided to leave. It sounds like the last decade of the twentieth century. While there is far more emphasis today on border control, borders are not absolute barriers to movement. Although governments try to control them, in fact people cross—and recross—national borders when they perceive that their lives are in danger.

Economic Causes

I miss my children terribly. They are six, five, and three years old.
I wish I could be with them, but I can't support them back home.
There are no jobs. I had to come here to find a job as a domestic
servant. It's hard work, but I can send money back home so that
my children can eat. No mother should be faced with such a
choice—to feed her children or live with them. My employer does-
n't even know I have children.

—Filipino domestic worker in Japan. From an interview with the
author, early 1990s. *A Moment to Choose: Risking to Be with
Uprooted People, A Resource Book.* Geneva: World Council of
Churches, 1997.

Historically, people have always tried to move when they
were unable to survive because of drought, famine, or widespread
unemployment. Poverty in the countryside spurs rural to urban
migration. This is true throughout the world. In China, the government estimates that there are now more than 100 million "sur-
plus farm laborers" who have migrated to the cities, with 15 million more arriving each year. By 2010, the government estimates
that half of China's population will live in cities, compared with
28 percent today and only 10 percent in the early 1980s.

Desperate economic conditions in the cities, in turn, may lead
people to move to other countries. But situations of extreme economic deprivation have not generated massive cross-border
migration. Rather, internal migration increases, and even when
people do leave their countries, the poorest are the last to leave.

Migration has become a key factor in the economies of many
regions. The Caribbean islands together send more migrants to the
United States than does any other country in the world, including
Mexico. Relatives working abroad send money home, and these
remittances are an important source of foreign exchange for many
countries. The World Bank estimates that remittances made by
migrant workers amounted to more than $65 billion a year at the
end of the 1980s—second only to crude oil in their value to the
world's economy.[1] This is an important source of hard currency
for governments of poor countries and helps reduce pressure on
already overstretched social services. For the families concerned,
it can mean the difference between survival and desperation.

Much of international migration occurs within regions. Thus, South Africa estimates that around 5 million migrants work within its borders—some legally, most without documents. This represents 12 percent of the country's total population, and the government is under pressure to expel the migrants in order to provide more jobs for South Africans. But many of the migrants are men who support their families in neighboring countries; and there is simply no work back home. Without the jobs in South Africa, their families could not survive.

Although people in Northern countries worry about the cost of immigrants to their societies, such migration has many negative consequences for the people of the sending countries as well. Approximately one-third of all African college graduates have left the continent, while almost 75 percent of doctors trained in Zaire and the Philippines work outside their countries. Not only does this mean that these countries are deprived of important human resources, but it also represents a transfer of wealth as countries of the North reap the benefits of investments in education made by countries of the South.

The facts of poverty are well known. More than a quarter of the world's people—between 1.2 and 1.3 billion human beings—live in absolute poverty. Nearly 2 billion lack safe drinking water. One of every three children born alive is undernourished at least some time during his or her first five years, and at least 14 million of those children die of hunger each year.

Poverty kills children as surely as do guns and landmines. In fact, poverty claims more victims than the fields of war. For the past five years, child deaths resulting from economic and social conditions have numbered a horrifying 8 to 9 million per year. In contrast, during 1992—a bad year for emergencies and conflicts—child deaths attributable to those emergencies probably amounted to between 500,000 and 1 million. Yet, the faces of the children suffering as a result of hunger—what UNICEF calls the "silent emergency"—are not on our television screens.

We know that poverty is the result of many factors: an unjust international economic system, greedy leaders, poor policies, international pressure, inequality at the national level, environmental degradation. We can identify those and other causes of poverty in specific situations, and we can name the enemies. But knowing the causes and developing effective strategies to confront them are two vastly different things.

The case of international debt is a clear example. By 1991, countries of the South had acquired a debt of about 1.3 trillion dollars—a figure representing approximately half of their combined gross national product and nearly twice their annual export earnings. Most of it was acquired between 1982 and 1990. The debt burden raises many issues, including the flow of resources between North and South, the human consequences of adjustment policies, responsibility for the debt, and the interaction between debt and war. But, in countries struggling to repay the debt—or interest on the debt—it is not governments that bear the main cost. Rather, it is the general population—people who had little say in acquiring the debt and who received no benefit from the loans. The fact that many of these loans were taken out by authoritarian governments, sometimes military rulers, is a bitter pill for countries seeking to re-establish democratic rule.

Moreover, the gap between North and South is widening. Between 1960 and 1989, the countries with the richest 20 percent of the world's population increased their share of the global gross national product (GNP) from 70.2 percent to 82.7 percent while those with the poorest 20 percent saw their share fall from 2.3 percent to 1.4 percent.[2] But, as has been clear for many years, poverty is not limited to countries of the South. Inequality in some wealthy countries, such as the United States, has increased dramatically in the last decade.

While deteriorating economic conditions may be a consequence of violence and governmental repression, economic underdevelopment in itself is not a major cause of refugee flows. Rather, it seems to be the interaction of economic and political factors that has caused most of the world's forced migration or uprooting. Refugee movements have historically tended to follow existing routes of economic migration. Thus, when the violence in El Salvador escalated in the early 1980s, hundreds of thousands of Salvadorans sought to escape by traveling to the United States— the traditional destination of economic migrants from their country. And, because of their large Salvadoran communities, cities such as Los Angeles became increasingly attractive destinations for refugees fleeing the violence of their homeland.

Environmental Causes

Environmental factors are clearly related to poverty, war, and migration. Millions of people have been forced to leave their communities because the land on which they live has become uninhabitable or is no longer able to support them. In some cases, the cause is a "natural" disaster; in others, the catastrophe is caused by humans. The disruption to the habitat may be sudden, as at Chernobyl or Bhopal, or gradual, as the spread of desert in the Sahara.

Destruction of our natural environment, including deforestation, loss of top soil, desertification, and degradation of agricultural land beyond restoration, is making traditional environments unlivable. An estimated 10 to 25 million people have been displaced for environmental reasons. Environmental damage causes poverty, but poverty also contributes to environmental degradation. People who have no alternatives cut down forests for fuel. Even when they know that their actions are going to make things worse in the long run, they have no other way to survive. This is also true for refugees. Malawi, for example, one of the poorest countries in Africa, was, for a decade, host to more than a million refugees from Mozambique. A consequence of this hospitality was the destruction of Malawi's forests. The refugees needed wood to cook their food and build their houses. They had nowhere else to turn.

Conflict over scarce natural resources is also an important cause of war. The deterioration of a natural resource base, coupled with demographic pressure and chronic poverty, can lead to or exacerbate political, ethnic, social, and economic tensions and, in turn, result in conflicts that force people to flee. And warfare does terrible things to the environment.

Political Factors

Since biblical times, governments have persecuted their citizens. Governments are becoming more sophisticated not only in their ability to launch widespread military campaigns against rural militants but also in the persecution of their opponents. The use of death squads and disappearances is a common way of eliminating political opposition. For years, the systematic repression of popular leaders in Guatemala, including leaders of trade unions, churches, and popular movements, prevented the development of effective opposition to the ruling elite. Entire social classes or ethnic groups, such as the professional classes in Cambodia under Pol Pot or the Kurds in Iraq under Saddam Hussein, may be presumed to hold political opinions in opposition to the state.

The violation of human rights—whether by governments persecuting individual opponents or during warfare—is the main cause of forced migration. Human rights violations are perhaps most obvious when governments persecute their opponents or discriminate against people of certain religious or ethnic backgrounds. But human rights include civil, economic, and cultural rights as well. When governments make policy decisions that prevent people from enjoying their basic human rights to education, economic self-sufficiency, and life itself, people often make the decision to uproot themselves and go somewhere else.

Since my late teens I was indirectly involved in the activities of my parents, brothers and sister in opposition to the regime at home. Six years ago my sister was arrested, one year later my parents and brothers. I never heard of any of them again. Following their disappearance, I took up the struggle for democracy. I quickly fell under suspicion and one night, as I was leaving the bakery where I worked, I was seized and thrust into a waiting car. I tried to escape at a traffic light but was shot in the leg.

Bleeding profusely and in great pain, I was blindfolded and taken to prison. There I was interrogated and beaten continuously for four or five hours. At first they beat me with their fists, then with a sort of steel-capped cudgel. When I started to lose consciousness, I was thrown into a cell [and the torture continued.] The following day I was again interrogated and taken to persuade women prisoners in the next cell to talk.

When the guards realized we were still not telling the truth, they took me to another room, tied me to a cross and poured petrol over me. I was left there for hours on end under threat of being burned alive. . . . When I was a little better, I was taken back to prison and tied up for hours in an unnatural position. Day after day, the torture continued. When I was again sent back to hospital, I realized that they did not want to kill me, just destroy me mentally and physically.

While I was in hospital, one of the nurses drugged my guards and helped me to escape. He brought me to the border, traveling by night and hiding by day.

—Torture victim in the Middle East. From *Resource Kit on Uprooted People, 1996*. Sydney: National Council of Churches in Australia.

Ethnic Conflicts

Most of today's nation-states are multiethnic, multinational creations. Although, currently, there are about four thousand different languages and perhaps five thousand different ethnic groups in the world, there are only 190 or so independent countries.

During the colonial period, colonizing powers often exploited local ethnic rivalries as a means of maintaining control. The political institutions they left behind when the colony became independent were usually unable to deal with the pressures of multiple ethnic demands. National boundaries, often set by colonial rulers, do not often correspond to lines of ethnic population distribution. When members of the ruling elite seek to strengthen national unity, they tend to turn on groups who do not fit in— those who are set apart by language, ethnicity, race, or religion.

Ethnic tensions are a fundamental cause of uprooting for several reasons. First, they are highly susceptible to political exploitation. Conflict is likely when one ethnic group is in power and uses that power to benefit its own group disproportionately. Factions seeking to mobilize support commonly try to inflame ethnic antagonisms for their own ends. Moreover, ethnic identity may be used as a defining characteristic of nationality. Claims for a Greater Serbia, for example, make clear that there is no place for a Bosnian Muslim or an ethnic Albanian. Members of groups other than the dominant one may be exposed first to discrimination, then to forced assimilation, persecution, expulsion, or even genocide.

Religion may play an important role in asserting ethnic identity. Thus, in the former Yugoslavia, the Serbian Orthodox Church is linked with Serbian nationalism, the Roman Catholic Church fuels Croatian nationalism, and Muslims are identified with Bosnian nationalists. Although there are many mixed marriages and situations in which individuals have stood firm against their own ethnic or religious group, religion is often deliberately used to promote ethnic loyalty.

War

Almost all of the world's ongoing armed conflicts are internal wars. Some are relatively recent, in places such as Tajikistan, Chechnya, Rwanda, and Burundi. In other places, such as Liberia,

Sri Lanka, and Angola, the wars have gone on for years or even decades. Deepening ethnic and religious tensions in countries such as Zaire, Nigeria, and India are clear warning signs that new outbreaks of civil violence may occur at any time. Typically, these conflicts begin over political disagreements, economic grievances, ethnic conflict, or religious differences. But, as the wars continue, they acquire their own dynamic of generalized violence. In Angola and Sierra Leone, Sri Lanka, and southern Sudan, armed groups ravage their countries and fight rival armed groups, creating a climate of terror and fear that has led to the displacement of millions of people. Civil strife has resulted in a breakdown of societal norms, and violence seems random. Power has passed into the hands of local warlords, and it becomes increasingly difficult to broker peace agreements

In these kinds of conflicts, mass population displacement has become an objective of the warring parties. The uprooting of 3 million people in the former Yugoslavia is not an unintended consequence of war. Rather, the point of the conflict is to force people to leave. In Rwanda, Burundi, Armenia, Azerbaijan, and Georgia, the forced displacement of populations is a central objective of the warring factions. Consequently, the numbers of people displaced in these conflicts are extraordinary. More than 50 percent—and perhaps as much as 80 percent—of Liberia's population has been displaced as the result of a war that has continued for seven years. The war in Somalia, which began in the early 1990s, produced 500,000 refugees and many more internally displaced people in a relatively short period of time. In Rwanda, half a million people were massacred in the first half of 1994, followed by an exodus of some 2 million refugees to Tanzania and Zaire, most of whom fled from their homeland in a single week. These sudden mass movements of people produce enormous strain on the international humanitarian system. As UNHCR says in *The State of the World's Refugees, 1996:* "While the number of refugee-producing conflicts has not increased significantly in recent years, the number of people displaced in each conflict has become much larger."

One of the most horrifying components of modern warfare is the extensive use of landmines. Landmines are a death sentence for thousands upon thousands of human beings. Even after conflicts have been resolved and warring armies have gone back to civilian life and turned in their weapons, landmines continue to claim lives for decades thereafter. Current estimates suggest that there are today 100 million landmines in sixty-four countries and 250,000 landmine-disabled people throughout the world. An additional 26,000 people become new landmine victims each year.

The direct medical and rehabilitation costs for the world's landmine victims are estimated at $750 million, and it will cost a minimum of $33 billion to clear the world of existing landmines (based on the dubious assumption that no new landmines will be laid).[3] However, the costs of landmines are far greater than even these figures indicate. For example, some kinds of landmines are deliberately designed to maim rather than kill their victims. This places a tremendous drain on medical resources and on family members who must care for their injured, often for extended periods. Although most mine victims are adult males, the impact of mines on families and children is substantial.

The presence of landmines clearly affects the displacement of the population. On the one hand, people leave areas that are heavily mined; on the other, the presence of mines complicates the return of refugees and internally displaced people. Refugees are afraid to go back to heavily mined areas, and the expense of mine awareness and mine clearance programs is an additional cost for repatriation schemes. Furthermore, there are serious long-term economic costs to a country when roads, bridges, dams, electrical installations, water supplies, and transportation infrastructure cannot be used because of landmines.

Civilian Casualties of War

Warring factions in the 1990s increasingly target civilians as casualties. This tendency is partly a result of increasingly sophisticated technology. Landmines, as noted, are a threat to civilian populations, and aerial bombardment has extended the potential battle zone to entire national territories. In conflicts within states, it is villages and suburban streets that are the new battlefields. Women and girls are particularly vulnerable to violence. In Rwanda, rape has been systematically used as a weapon of ethnic cleansing in order to destroy community ties. In some raids, virtually every adolescent girl who survived an attack by the militia was subsequently raped. Many who became pregnant were ostracized by their families and communities. Some abandoned their babies; others committed suicide.

> **He shall judge between the nations, and shall arbitrate for many peoples; they shall beat their swords into plowshares, and their spears into pruning hooks; nation shall not lift up sword against nation, neither shall they learn war anymore. Isa. 2:4.**

UNICEF has analyzed the impact of today's warfare on children, concluding that families and children are also being targeted as a result of ethnic conflict, since a "perilous logic" clicks in when ethnic loyalties prevail. "The escalation from ethnic superiority to ethnic cleansing to genocide can become an irresistible process. Killing adults is then not enough; future generations of the enemy—their children—must also be eliminated. As one political commentator said in a 1994 radio broadcast before violence erupted in Rwanda, 'To kill the big rats, you have to kill the little rats.'"[4]

A grenade had landed on our shelter. We had to climb over the dead bodies to get out. Meanwhile, the snipers kept shooting at us. My father was one of those wounded and was taken away to the hospital. We've not seen him since, but I hope that he is still alive, perhaps in one of the detention camps. I try not to talk about these things, but I get so upset and keep having nightmares about what happened.

—Kazimir, age 13. From "Children in the Former Yugoslavia," *The State of the World's Children, 1996,* p. 15. New York: UNICEF, 1996.

This violence has an obvious long-term impact on children—and on the future reconstruction of their countries. Children are the innocent victims of violence. But, beyond that, they are increasingly being drawn into the wars as soldiers. The proliferation of light weapons, the forced recruitment of ever younger children, the large number of orphans, and the greater availability of drugs have meant an increase in the number of child soldiers. As conflicts drag on for years, fighting becomes their way of life—and often looting and raping, as well. Once a peace agreement is signed, even after troops are demobilized, the reintegration of child soldiers into the fabric of normal life is a daunting task. A worker in a nongovernmental organization who has years of experience with child soldiers in Sierra Leone observed that it is not just a question of putting these kids back with their loving families. Fighting, he said, has become their preferred way of life, and the rewards of power, money, recognition, and belonging which they get from the gangs are hard to replicate in normal life.

Economic Consequences of War

Armed conflicts produce substantial economic benefits to arms traders and manufacturers. They also bring with them serious economic costs for the victims of war. Most immediately, wars kill people or displace them from their homes. In either case, the human resources of a country or region are seriously damaged. Agricultural production typically plummets as people are forced to abandon their farms. Less food is available, so the cost of local produce goes up. Rural people flock to the cities, but there are no jobs available there, either, since urban employment suffers as a consequence of war. The economic and social infrastructure is often devastated, with factories destroyed and transportation and communications networks rendered unusable. Unemployment in Bosnia, for example, is estimated at more than 70 percent. The long-term economic effects of closed schools and deteriorating health services are enormous. Government funds intended for social spending and economic investment are used to pay for armies and counterinsurgency campaigns.

When combined with the debt—from borrowed funds often used to purchase arms to continue the war—economic costs of war are mammoth. In El Salvador in the early 1990s, 41 percent of the government's budget went for servicing the foreign debt, and an additional 26 percent was spent on the military. So, 67 percent of the government's resources was devoted to debt and war. The Philippine government spent 44 percent on external debt service and 12 percent on the military, for a total cost of 56 percent of the government's budget.[5] Those are resources that cannot then be used to improve the social and economic well-being of the Salvadoran and Filipino people. The usual pattern is for governments of countries with internal conflict to borrow heavily for military spending—often to buy arms from the five countries that are the permanent members of the United Nations Security Council.

Armed conflicts have a dramatic impact on the general health of the population, as well. The effects go far beyond maiming by bullets. Most casualties of war are caused by disease and famine. In Somalia during 1992, half or more of all children under five years old on 1 January were dead by 31 December—and approximately 90 percent of them died from malnutrition and disease. War interrupts the distribution of food, destroys agricultural land, and ruins the infrastructure, such as, for example, the means of providing safe water. In Mozambique between 1982 and 1986, more than 40 percent of health centers were destroyed. In Uganda between 1972 and 1985, half the doctors and 80 percent of the pharmacists abandoned the country in search of better opportunities elsewhere.

The causes of uprooting are complex. Some people leave because of ethnic cleansing or individual persecution while others flee desperate economic or environmental catastrophes. Most typically, however, there is no single clear-cut cause but rather a somewhat untidy interplay of many factors. In 1984, for example, a terrible famine hit Ethiopia and millions of people were displaced. But the famine was not just the natural consequence of drought or other climatic conditions. Rather, it was the result of policies imposed by the military dictator, General Mengistu Haile Mariam. Conditions became infinitely worse because of policies that he implemented, causing massive displacement, starvation, and death.

In 1992, a severe drought affected southern Africa. Throughout the region, animals died from lack of water, and food production plummeted. But there was no widespread starvation and no displacement of millions of people. The international community reacted quickly, moving food to people where they were, so they did not have to flee. Affected governments allowed access to all regions of their country. Even in Mozambique, still in the process of negotiating an end to its sixteen-year-old conflict, the warring factions agreed to let assistance reach their people in need. Drought does not have to mean famine or displacement of people. Nor do other natural disasters. Within the space of a few months, earthquakes of roughly similar intensity hit northern California and Armenia. Four people died in San Francisco; in

Armenia, casualties numbered in the thousands. Poverty always makes the effects of natural calamities worse.

To explore the relationships between these different causal factors, we will now examine one of the most tragic cases of forced uprooting in recent years: Rwanda.

UGANDA

Goma•

RWANDA

Kigali •

ZAIRE

BURUNDI

•Bujumbura

TANZANIA

THREE

Rwanda, Center of a Maelstrom

In April 1994, a bloodbath of monumental proportions broke out in Rwanda. More than 800,000 people were killed—most with machetes, mostly by neighbors. Thousands were killed by grenades or fires as they sought shelter within churches. During a single two-day period that month, 250,000 refugees poured into Tanzania—the largest number of refugees in recent history to move in such a short time span. Three months later, more than a million refugees crossed into Zaire during the course of a single week. News broadcasts at the time spoke of ten thousand people an hour pouring into Zaire. Think about the numbers. Ten thousand people an hour! Where would they go? Where would they sleep? What would they eat?

Although international institutions had not been able to prevent the violence, and, in fact, had reduced peacekeeping forces at precisely the moment when they were most needed, aid poured into Zaire and Tanzania afterwards to help the refugees. But much of it was too late for those who had arrived in that initial influx. Close to fifty thousand refugees died in Goma, Zaire, as the international community struggled to respond to this humanitarian crisis.

After two and a half years in camps, most of the 1.7 million refugees returned home. Rwandan refugees in Zaire left quickly, almost spontaneously, when the camps were attacked by Rwandan forces, and military leaders in the camps lost their power over the people who lived there. Within a month, some 700,000 refugees had simply begun to walk home—although conditions in Rwanda were still very unsettled. Another 300,000 to 500,000 Rwandan refugees fled deeper into Zaire, where they walked for months in search of assistance. But conditions had degenerated so much with increased fighting by rebels who claimed a third of Zairian territory, that it was difficult to bring help to refugees on the move. In fact, it was difficult for UNHCR just to find the refugees in eastern Zaire's dense forests. In neighboring Tanzania, the repatriation of Rwandan refugees from Zaire led the government to declare that all Rwandan refugees in Tanzania would have to return home by the end of 1996. When the refugees protested that they were afraid to return home, the Tanzanian government sent military troops into the camps to force the refugees to go back.

The story of the Rwandan emergency illustrates many of the interconnected causes of the violence—economic, political, environmental, and ethnic. The response of the international community to the immediate disaster also shows remarkably shortsighted—and generous—responses by governments far from Central Africa. Unfortunately, the years since the April 1994 bloodbath also demonstrate how a conflict in one country can have repercussions in others. Although this chapter focuses largely on Rwanda, similar patterns of tension and violence are evident in Burundi and eastern Zaire. In both countries, conflicts between Hutus and Tutsis have escalated in the aftermath of the Rwandan bloodbath. Clearly, there is no easy way to prevent genocide in Burundi or massacres in Zaire, but one profound lesson to be learned by the international community from the Rwandan tragedy is the value of taking some risks to prevent mass violence and killing.

What might have happened in Rwanda if the estimated US $2 billion spent on refugee relief in the first two weeks of the emergency had been devoted to keeping the peace, protecting human rights and promoting development in the period which preceded the exodus?

—From *The State of the World's Refugees, 1996*, p. 239. Geneva: UNHCR.

A Troubled Past

Most accounts of the Rwandan conflict start with the ethnic hatred between that country's majority Hutu and minority Tutsi populations. Deeply rooted in the region's colonial past and exacerbated by economic and environmental pressures, the ethnic conflict was deliberately manipulated by political leaders on both sides. For almost four hundred years, the Tutsis had been the traditional rulers of the Hutus—a pattern reinforced by Belgium when it ruled Rwanda as a colony from 1919 to 1960 and introduced forced labor. The Belgians chose the Tutsis to administer the fields and the Hutus to work as manual laborers. What limited educational opportunities existed went to Tutsis; Hutus were seen as a permanent underclass. Although they constituted only 9 percent of Rwanda's population, Tutsis were the elite. All Rwandan leaders appointed by the Belgians were called "traditional chiefs," (though they may have been nothing of the sort) and all were Tutsis. They controlled all institutions and held most of the country's wealth.

The Belgians also introduced ethnic registration, which meant that a person's ethnic identity was stamped on his or her identity card. Since the physical differences between Hutus and Tutsis are not decisive, and since they speak the same language and practice the same religions, the Belgians developed dubious criteria to make these distinctions, including nose width (measured in millimeters) and occupation. For example, they classified individuals owning more than ten cows as Tutsi, regardless of ethnic parentage. Although generally such classifications were based on economic rather than ethnic or racial criteria, once made, they were set in stone. A person's identity, social networks, political opinions, and opportunities were shaped in large measure by his or her ethnic classification.

After World War II, as Rwanda moved toward independence, the Belgians changed their policy. Instead of favoring Tutsis as the elite, they began to name Hutus to positions of power. The pressure was on to create democracies; rule by an ethnic group representing only 9 percent of the population was no longer viable. But the Belgian flip-flop had its costs. Tutsis were desperate to hang on to their position of privilege, while Hutus aggressively asserted their newly acquired power. New local Hutu chiefs and political leaders began to persecute Tutsis. Successive Rwandan governments and opposition political leaders exploited fears of ethnic domination for their own political ends. Outbreaks of ethnic violence became more common, and Tutsis fled to neighboring countries, starting a cycle of violence that has continued to the present day. For thirty years, the refugees in exile would organize small military bands that invaded Rwanda, seeking to restore the Tutsis to their former position of power. The Hutus would retaliate and force them back into exile. In the process, many people died and many spent decades as refugees.

The granting of formal independence to Rwanda in 1962 did not fundamentally change the situation. In December 1963, Tutsi refugees launched an attack from Burundi that was followed by Hutu reprisals and the massacre of ten thousand Tutsis. By 1964, UNHCR estimated that more than 150,000 Rwandan refugees were in neighboring countries, mostly in those where they had ethnic kin. Even as periodic attacks would be launched from refugee camps, the refugees dreamed of coming home. But successive Rwandan governments created obstacles to their return.

Nevertheless, the violence in Rwanda is more than a product of deep ethnic tensions. Rwanda is a small landlocked country, about the size of Maryland or Belgium, with the highest population density in Africa and an annual population growth rate of more than 3 percent. The pressure on the land is enormous, because most of the people rely on subsistence agriculture for survival and only 6 percent of the population lives in cities. Since independence, the country's limited agricultural land has been divided into increasingly smaller plots. Land-hungry people have encroached on forests, and ever more intensive use of the land is depleting it of its nutrients, causing it to become less productive. In the decade of the 1980s, Rwanda experienced a 30 percent reduction in per capita food production. The country's main export crops, traditionally coffee and tea, accounted for 80 percent of its exports. But in 1987, the International Coffee Agreement collapsed, and the price of Rwandan coffee fell to half of its 1980 level.

Throughout the 1980s, Rwanda's economy was in trouble. The GNP fell by an annual rate of 2.4 percent per capita, and the nation's total foreign debt increased from $189 million to $844 million.[1] Thousands of Rwandans sought better economic prospects through migration—a traditional response to economic problems in the country. In 1990, the World Bank insisted that Rwanda put into place a structural adjustment program, freezing public salaries and devaluing the local currency by almost 80 percent. The stage was set.

Rwanda
(pre-crisis)

Population: . . . . .7.8 million
Language: . . . . .Kinyarwanda, French
Ethnic groups: . . . . .Hutu: 90% of the population
 . . . . .Tutsi: 9% of the population
 . . . . .Twa: 1% of the population
Religions: . . . . .Roman Catholic: 65%
 . . . . .Traditional Beliefs: 17%
 . . . . .Protestant: 9%
 . . . . .Muslim: 9%
Capital city: . . . . .Kigali
GNP per capita: $210
Infant mortality rate: 80%
Life expectancy: . . . . .47 years
Adult literacy: 54%
Percent urban: 6

—From *The Rwandan Refugee Crisis.* Geneva: World Council of Churches, 1994.

The War Begins

During neighboring Uganda's civil war, thousands of Rwandan refugees fought with the rebel forces of Yoweri Museveni, now president of Uganda, planning their own return to Rwanda and acquiring military expertise in the process. In October 1990 (ironically just a few months after Hutu President Juvenal Habyarimana agreed to introduce multiparty politics in

Rwanda), a force of four thousand Rwandan rebels entered Rwanda through Uganda. Calling themselves the Rwandan Patriotic Front (RPF), the rebels, overwhelmingly Tutsi, insisted that their goal was not reimposing Tutsi domination, but, rather, forcing the government to share power. Few Hutus believed them.

The invasion had immediate consequences. Overnight, ethnic tensions increased dramatically. Tutsis were viewed as supporting the invasion, and President Habyarimana set up a new political party—the Coalition for the Defense of the Republic (CDR)—which openly advocated Hutu supremacy. Like all governments facing military threat, the Rwandan government became more repressive, cracking down on all opponents and violating human rights on a large scale.

The president also moved quickly to build up the country's armed forces. In October 1990, when the war broke out, the military numbered about five thousand; by 1992, it had grown to thirty thousand. Training was minimal, unemployed young men were recruited off the streets, and, as might be expected, the level of human rights abuses was high. But President Habyarimana went a step further and urged extremist political parties to form paramilitary groups. These groups carried out raids on Tutsis and operated radio stations that blared out propaganda, exacerbating ethnic hatred. In countries where literacy rates are low, radio broadcasts are the primary source of information; in Rwanda, these broadcasts played on the fears of a populace under military attack and a nation suffering economic decline. The growth in the military forces was also costly, leading to increased debt and fewer resources for social services or development. However, in spite of the escalating violence and the government's lack of cash, there were few difficulties in securing the necessary arms from South Africa and, particularly, France. These two nations provided the Rwandan government with approximately $12 million in arms of all kinds.

But in spite of the government's military buildup, the RPF continued to win victories, and international pressure increased on the Rwandan government to work out a cease-fire. In 1993, the RPF and President Habyarimana signed an agreement, known as the Arusha Accords, mandating a series of far-reaching political reforms to end the war. The UN Security Council agreed to send peacekeeping troops—the United Nations Assistance Mission for

Rwanda (UNAMIR)—with a mandate to monitor the cease-fire, provide for security in the country, repatriate refugees, clear mines, and coordinate humanitarian assistance. The first UN forces arrived in Kigali in October 1993. Their mandate was to remain in Rwanda for six months.

In spite of the peace agreement, radio propaganda continued and escalated. The CDR, the party associated with the president, not only extolled Hutu supremacy, but openly called on Hutus to kill Tutsi civilians. Paramilitary groups began to attack human rights activists as well as those moderate Hutus who were urging reconciliation and restraint. Death lists circulated and people were afraid.

In addition to the tense climate in Rwanda, similar ethnic tensions played themselves out in neighboring Burundi. On 21 October 1993, there was an attempted coup which resulted in the assassination of President Ndadaye and six members of his cabinet. "Hutus went on the offensive, binding their Tutsi neighbors with ropes and hacking them to death. Vengeful Tutsi soldiers, given carte blanche by their commanders, marched into Hutu villages causing tens of thousands of Hutu peasants to flee from their villages and fields. Many (including women, children and infants) were hacked or burnt to death. In Bujumbura alone, 4,000 were loaded on trucks and taken to their graves. In secondary and technical schools, scores of Hutu students were beaten to death.

"Relief organizations compelled to seek out the wounded in isolated regions reported entire villages aflame and rivers choked with bloated bodies in the central and northern parts of Burundi. Almost one tenth of the Burundian population (273,000) fled to Rwanda, 250,000 to Tanzania and 40,000 to Zaire. According to the International Committee of the Red Cross estimates, up to 100,000 people were killed and some 206,000 displaced in Burundi."
—From *UNHCR Fact Sheet*, 25 July 1994.

The signs were clear that violence was increasing. The United Nations, whose troops in Rwanda then numbered about 2,500, was concerned. UN Secretary-General Boutros Boutros-Ghali's report of 30 March 1994 noted that since December "the security situation in Rwanda, and especially in Kigali, has seriously deteriorated. While most incidents can be attributed to armed banditry, which has been growing as a result of the ready availability of weapons, ethnic and politically motivated crimes, including assassinations and murders, have also increased."

A Plane Crash—and Genocide

On 6 April 1994, an airplane carrying Rwandan President Habyarimana and Burundian President Ntaryamira back from negotiations in Tanzania crashed at the Kigali airport. Everyone was killed. The response was immediate. Hutu extremists charged that Tutsis were responsible for killing their president and went on a rampage. Within hours of the news, checkpoints were set up around Kigali and cars were stopped and searched. Hutu militants dragged out the Tutsis, killed them, and left their bodies piled on the roadsides. The paramilitary groups searched out both Tutsi leaders and moderate Hutu politicians and intellectuals, and killed them and their families. The violence quickly spread to the countryside. International staff of UN and nongovernmental organizations was evacuated. Commercial flights in and out of the country were suspended. Frantic telephone calls from frightened individuals and propaganda from partisan radio stations became the primary sources of news about the terror.

On 20 April, the UN Secretary-General bluntly reported to the Security Council that with the deteriorating situation, the previous mandate of UNAMIR no longer applied. He pointed out that the choice was clear: the UN could beef up its forces and extend its mandate to prevent further violence; it could sharply reduce its forces to 270 troops to assist with only humanitarian relief and try to get a cease-fire; or it could withdraw its troops completely. At the very moment that the conflict was escalating, the member states of the Security Council voted to pull back from the idea of further engagement. The memories of UN troops in Somalia were still fresh. It was eventually agreed to reduce the number of UN troops to 270 soldiers and to limit their activities. UNAMIR could monitor the situation, encourage the parties to work for a cease-fire, and resume humanitarian activities where possible, but it was not authorized to use force for prevention of violence. The UNAMIR forces did a reasonably good job of protecting the fifteen thousand Rwandans who sought protection in the UN compound. But they did not stop the killing.

Massacres occurred throughout the entire country. Hutu paramilitary troops went from door to door, killing all Tutsis as well as many Hutus who opposed the slaughter. Whole villages populated by Tutsis were completely destroyed. Thousands and thousands of Tutsis ran for protection to churches—where they were killed en masse by paramilitary forces. Grenades were thrown through church doors, and machetes were used to finish the killing. No one—not children, women, the elderly, babies—was spared. This was not a war between armies; it was a war between neighbors. Most of the victims knew their killers.

Propaganda by Hutu extremists and the government had done its job well. Many Hutus fervently believed that the only way to ensure their survival was to kill every single Tutsi in the country. Estimates of the number of people who participated in the killing range from thirty thousand to 100,000. Some later explained that to refuse would have meant their own deaths. Yet, even in the midst of the genocide, there were cases of Hutus hiding Tutsi families and helping them to escape. Many moderate Hutus were targeted and killed by the extremists because they refused to be swept up in the anti-Tutsi hysteria. In the words of one Rwandan pastor, "The only way to explain what happened, with neighbor killing neighbor, with pastors exhorting their congregations to kill each other, is to say that evil was loose in the land."

My God, my God, why have you forsaken me? Why are you so far from helping me, from the words of my groaning? O my God, I cry by day, but you do not answer; and by night, but find no rest. Ps. 22:1-2.

As news of the massacres—now recognized as genocide—swept forth, the Tutsi-dominated Rwandan Patriotic Front began to move toward Kigali. The RPF had been in the process of beginning to demobilize as specified under the peace agreement, but the situation had now changed. So, at the same time that the slaughter was going on in Hutu-controlled areas, the RPF was fighting a more conventional type of war against government troops. As the RPF forces approached, Hutus feared a bloodbath of revenge at the hands of the Tutsis.

Thousands of people fled their communities. More than 250,000 Rwandan refugees flooded into Tanzania between 28 and 29 April in the largest, fastest exodus UNHCR has ever seen. Almost all the refugees were Hutus fleeing the approaching RPF army. Among them was a small but significant number of extremist Hutu military leaders—a fact that was to complicate the bringing of relief to the refugees. The Kagera River, which separates Tanzania and Rwanda, was congested with floating bodies—some of them mutilated and decapitated—providing the clearest possible sign that the violence continued.

The UN Acts

By the end of April 1994, aid organizations feared that 200,000 Rwandans had been killed. Almost all of the agencies had been forced to evacuate their personnel. Boutros Boutros-Ghali asked for a strong new UN force with a mandate to protect threatened civilians. But there was opposition by some powerful countries, particularly the United States, to sending in peacekeeping troops. The United States sought to play down the scale of the crisis. By some accounts, it was reluctant to acknowledge that what was happening in Rwanda was genocide, because as a signatory to the UN's Convention on Genocide, it would be compelled to take action.

After weeks of wrangling, the members of the UN Security Council agreed to send a scaled-down, limited UNAMIR-II force. But there were delays in actually implementing the decision. Then, in mid-June, with no new UN forces present, France (with its strong geopolitical interest in the francophone countries of Central Africa) suddenly announced that it was sending 2,500 troops to set up a safe zone, known as Operation Turquoise, to protect civilians. Although the French troops established a secure zone in the southwestern part of Rwanda, they found, when they arrived, that most of the region's Tutsi population had already been murdered. People displaced from their communities found a measure of security in the French zone, but, like internally displaced people everywhere, their lives were on hold.

In a largely forgotten corner of this tiny, devastated nation, the survivors of drought, massacres, and war are now facing the ravages of malnutrition and starvation.

At a makeshift refugee camp for tens of thousands of people living in crude huts on steep slopes, tiny Albert Uwamahoro . . . is one year old. He weighs 12 pounds. His father, a Tutsi, and an older brother and sister were killed in April by a Hutu mob. He was spared because his mother, who was carrying him, is a member of Rwanda's Hutu ethnic majority.

Nearby, five-year-old Habirora sits listlessly, his bulging eyes staring vacantly. He weighs 21 pounds. His family fled their village in eastern Rwanda in May. "Because of the war," says his mother, who has not eaten in a day and to survive at all over the last three months has sold goats, kitchenware and her clothes. "I have nothing left to sell," she said.

While the world focuses on the misery of one million Rwandans who poured into Zaire last month and struggled with death and disease, the plight of the refugees in the southwestern region [of Rwanda] has steadily worsened. Most began arriving three months ago to escape a civil war and ethnic massacres in the east.

No one here knows for sure how many displaced people there are in this corner of Rwanda, where the French established a "safe haven" measuring 50 by 90 miles in July. Estimates range from 350,000 to 750,000 refugees; most are encamped in an area occupying about a third of the zone. . . .

To survive, Mrs. Mukahigiro has been forced to sell the few things she managed to carry when she fled her village in May. "I have sold all my clothes except this," she said, tugging at a long, tattered piece of cloth she has wrapped around her. "I sold my blanket and my head scarf and three plates," she said. She said her husband had also sold his clothes.

—From "Starvation Threatens a Rwanda 'Safe Haven'," by Raymond Bonner, *New York Times*, 7 August 1994.

By mid-July, the RPF forces were advancing from the north and thousands of Hutus were fleeing their approach, fearing reprisals by the Tutsis for Hutu violence. Meanwhile, the international community set up operations to care for hundreds of thousands of Rwandan refugees in Tanzania; hundreds of thousands of displaced Rwandans lived in temporary camps throughout Rwanda. Just when it seemed that it could not get worse, it did.

The Tragedy of Goma

A million refugees crossed into Zaire about 14 July 1994 near a small town called Goma—at a rate of ten thousand people an hour. They had been running and walking for days, trying to reach the border before the Tutsi-dominated RPF forces caught up with them. They were tired, hungry, thirsty, and weak. In the chaos of the moment—trying to deal with ten thousand people an hour pouring into the country—poor choices were made about where to set up the refugee sites. Because Goma town was overcrowded, refugees were sent north of the city to an area without available water. Nor was there water available between Goma and the spot to which the refugees were directed. Many died after they arrived in Zaire, while walking to the proposed refugee site. The camp was situated on volcanic rock where it was impossible to drill wells, meaning that every drop of water had to be trucked in. The U.S. government responded by sending military forces to set up water purification and water delivery systems. But in spite of monumental efforts, during the early weeks of the crisis as many as two thousand people died each day. This declined in a few months to three hundred per day. But lack of coordination, scale of the influx, and lack of water at the site cost 46,000 lives. Up to 100,000 refugees and internally displaced people died during the refugee outflows.

Significantly, in the chaos of the moment no effort was made to separate armed extremists from civilian refugees. However, even if UNHCR and the Zairian government had wanted to do so, they were confronted with the reality of a well-armed group of people who were desperate to remain in Zaire with the refugees. The failure to separate the "intimidators" (as they were called) meant that the refugee camps came to be under the de facto control of the extremists.

Kibumba is a camp 28 kilometers north of the town of Goma, Zaire. It is the most populous of all the Rwandan refugee camps in the area, and it is the farthest from a clean water source. . . . In most such refugee emergencies in Africa, the death rates are highest among children under five. In this situation, the death rate is high among this group, but due to the physical endurance and strength required by adults to survive this situation, the death rate among adults is equally high. This has caused a serious problem: orphans. Mothers literally work themselves to death trying to care for their families. They lie down and die, leaving their children sitting next to their dead bodies. Usually the children are so confused they do not understand for many hours that their mothers are dead nor what to do about the situation when they realize they are alone. Often the children sit next to their mothers' bodies for days before they either wander off or lie down and die next to them.

The camp is so densely populated that from a few meters away one cannot see the ground between the people at all, only the mass of people. The air smells of dead bodies. It is dusty from all the people walking and is smoky and sticky from all the wood fires. There is a low rumble of people talking sharply to one another. Almost never does anyone laugh or cry. When the refugees do greet each other, they say "Be strong."

—Barbara Smith. From *Women's Commission News,* Women's Commission for Refugee Women and Children, International Rescue Committee, New York, February 1994.

Meanwhile, back in Rwanda, the RPF took control of the country in July and announced the formation of a transitional government, with Hutus as both president and prime minister. The French troops withdrew. The new government announced that the refugees were welcome to return and that there would be no reprisals. But the refugees were afraid to go home. They were uncertain about their fate in Rwanda. Furthermore, extremist leaders in the camps threatened to kill any refugees who expressed interest in returning.

The Repatriation Dilemma

By July 1994, UNHCR was assisting 2.1 million Rwandan refugees in four countries: Rwanda, Burundi, Zaire, and Uganda. The organization was also caring for 600,000 Burundian refugees and returnees. More than half of all Rwandans were either dead, displaced, or living as refugees. From the very beginning of the refugee crisis, international agencies began planning for the return of the refugees. Repatriation was the only solution for the grim conditions facing the people in the camps, as well as for Rwanda's neighbors, who were becoming increasingly impatient with the presence of millions of refugees in their midst.

The refugee camps were not good places for people to live, and there were immediate security problems. The influx of refugees—mainly Hutus fleeing the RPF advance in the country— included thousands of people implicated in the killings. Leaders of the Hutu paramilitary groups sought to assert control of the camps, intimidating people, taking food supplies, and using every opportunity to denounce and weaken the new Rwandan government.

The Rwandan government, meanwhile, wanted the refugee camps closed, since their presence on the country's borders was clearly perceived as a military threat. In 1995 and early 1996, attacks were launched from exiled Rwandan groups against a government which, itself, had come to power through a military force formed among refugees living in exile.

But the return of the refugees depended on reestablishing peace and stability in Rwanda. The UN deployed human-rights monitors throughout the country, hoping that their presence might reassure the refugees that Rwanda was safe for them. But the number of monitors was very small, and in late 1996 renewed violence and the murder of four human rights monitors caused the others to be withdrawn from rural areas. Moreover, the UN began scaling down its UNAMIR peacekeeping forces, and in March 1996 the last UN troops withdrew from the country.

From the very beginning, the Rwandan government was determined to bring all perpetrators to justice. The UN Security Council established the International Criminal Tribunal for Rwanda to prosecute those who had committed genocide and other crimes against humanity. But the process has been very slow; few indictments have been issued, and the court proceedings are not seen as fair. The judicial system in Rwanda has been largely destroyed; as many as 80 percent of the country's police and judicial force have died or are in exile. Collecting evidence and statements from witnesses and actually carrying out the trials is extraordinarily difficult. Thus, people suspected of participating in the killing were placed in prisons to await investigation and judicial action. By mid-1997, more than ninety thousand men, women, and children suspected of participating in the 1994 genocide were being held in Rwandan prisons and detention centers. Conditions were appalling, since the prisons were originally designed to support only ten thousand people. More than two thousand prisoners have died in the horribly overcrowded cells. Some refugees are still afraid to return to Rwanda for fear of being detained in those prisons, perhaps indefinitely.

Land has been another major issue. Returning Tutsi refugees occupied the land and dwellings of Hutus who had fled. While the government said this was a temporary provision, and that when the Hutus returned the Tutsis would be moved elsewhere, questions remained about who would pay for the moves and where the Tutsis would go. Still another obstacle relates to inheritance laws. Under Rwandan law, women cannot inherit property. This means that a woman whose husband was killed in the violence has no right to occupy their home. Given the large number of widows in today's Rwanda, this is a serious problem, one that prevents women from returning to their communities. Finally, the prevalence of landmines throughout some areas of Rwanda limits the regions to which refugees can return. The landmines also mean that reconstruction in Rwanda will have to include either demining (which is terribly expensive) or mine-awareness programs for people returning to affected areas.

The security situation in Goma and other Zairian towns bordering Rwanda is extremely precarious. Ethnic strife in Rwanda and the huge refugee influx into Zaire have badly affected the socio-economic life in eastern Zaire. The situation in Goma is chaotic. Rwandan government forces have been completely routed and thousands of troops have fled with the refugees into Goma, bringing large quantities of arms which the Zairian authorities are trying to confiscate, but they too have been overwhelmed by the size of the influx. Ethnic tension in the town is rising. There have been reports of Zairian soldiers harassing refugees, and aid workers are trying to transfer the refugees to refugee camps outside the town as quickly as possible. UNHCR officials are concerned about assisting an army in exile in a separate camp, and about reports that vanquished government troops are regrouping to carry out attacks against the RPF. An estimated 40,000 soldiers are in the region, and UNHCR has received reports that these soldiers are robbing refugees, including orphans, and frightening aid workers in refugee camps.

The Goma area has Hutu-Tutsi hostilities of its own, which claimed thousands of lives in 1993. Aid workers fear that the influx of Hutu refugees may well incite a new rash of violence. The UN Secretary-General fears the whole region will be threatened if the mass exodus does not stop.

—From *UNHCR Fact Sheet,* 25 July 1994.

On the economic front, things look more optimistic. International financial institutions report that the Rwandan economy is recovering well. It is expected to reach 5 percent real growth in 1996, and reports are that the economy recovered by almost 40 percent in 1995. But the devastation wrought by war is matched only by incredible hatred and fear. Lack of human resources is a real obstacle. The services of some 80 percent of the country's police force and judicial officials, as previously noted, and a majority of teachers and other government workers were lost to the refugee exodus and genocide. Even as the Rwandan government struggles with reconstruction, some believe that too many resources were devoted to the refugees, and too few were used to help rebuild the country so that refugees could return with some expectation of resuming their lives.

One of the biggest obstacles to repatriation was the presence in the camps of soldiers from the former army and paramilitary groups who pressured the refugees not to return. There were wild rumors about the Rwandan government's plans to revenge the slaughter by killing returning refugees. Military leaders used physical intimidation to prevent the refugees from choosing to return.

The presence of over 2 million refugees in Rwanda's neighboring countries had enormous economic, environmental, and political costs, and from the beginning it was recognized that repatriation of the refugees was central to the region's recovery. In the early days of the crisis, the moral dilemma for humanitarian agencies was whether to send people home or encourage them to stay in refugee camps without adequate water and with death rates that were very high. But soon the pressure to send refugees home came from host governments that were not only reeling under the strain of caring for millions of people, but were also concerned about the possibility of violence, serious economic consequences, and environmental devastation.

The environmental consequences to these neighboring host countries have been tremendous. By 1995, refugees living in the largest camp in Tanzania had to walk approximately 12 kilometers—more than 5 miles—to reach the nearest source of firewood. Much of the pastureland near the camps has been seriously overgrazed by the thousands of animals the refugees brought with them. According to UNHCR, the Rwandan crisis "has caused irreversible damage to the vegetation in Zaire's Virunga national park, a UNESCO World Heritage site. According to one UNHCR estimate, some 800,000 kilograms of wood and grass were being collected from the park by refugees each day in December 1994, a level which evidently cannot be sustained if the unique flora and fauna found in the area are to be conserved."[2]

The population of Goma, Zaire, grew from 20,000 to 250,000 almost overnight. Local unemployment skyrocketed since Rwandan refugees, who received food rations, could afford to work for less than the local Zairian population. At the same time, the price of all local goods increased dramatically. Epidemics of cholera and other diseases in the camps harmed Zairians as well. These factors intensified the effects of Zaire's own years of political turmoil and ethnic strife. The refugees sold arms to local Zairians, contributing to the militarization of local conflicts. Almost 10,000 Zairians of Tutsi origin fled to Rwanda in late 1995 and early 1996, seeking safety from attacks by armed Hutu militias. The local Zairian population wanted the Rwandan refugees to go home.

Burundi also has troubles, with escalation of political violence and increasing fear of a genocide like that which occurred in Rwanda. Periodic fighting, confirmed massacres, and widespread human-rights violations have pushed Burundi to the brink of all-out war. Rwandan refugees who sought protection in Burundi were forced by the Burundian government to return, or left on their own in search of security elsewhere. The escalation of violence in Burundi means that the country is not safe for Rwandan refugees—or for its own population. As the fighting has intensified inside Burundi during the past year, Burundians have been uprooted from their communities. The government insists that internally displaced people be put into special camps for protection; but many believe that living in camps actually increases their vulnerability to violence by making them more visible.

While UNHCR and local governments were thus planning for the repatriation of the refugees and trying to set up programs to convince them that it was safe to return, nongovernmental organizations (NGOs) set up assistance programs in the camps. More than 170 international NGOs flocked to the region in the aftermath of the tragedy. Even though local churches and smaller NGOs were the first to respond to the needs of the refugees, they have been largely neglected by the big international NGOs that drive up the salaries, lure away experienced workers, and have much better equipment. Nevertheless, some excellent programs have been developed. For example, through the efforts of such organizations as Save the Children, the International Committee of the Red Cross, and others, one of the largest tracing systems in the world has reunited some forty thousand Rwandan children with their families.

We had planned to have an ecumenical service in Kinuaranda today, but we had not made very solid arrangements. Esperence had told a number of people and thought that we might have 50 or so. We borrowed a small chapel for the occasion, and bought bread and tea to share with the participants after the service. As we went to prepare the chapel, we found more than 500 people waiting (!) and so immediately changed our plans, and prepared a place outside. (We also abandoned the idea of tea and bread, and ran out to buy peanuts!) Sam preached as "a refugee to refugees, as someone hurt to those hurting, as someone with hope to those who had no hope," and others gave testimonies of how they had coped, how they had been saved by those of the opposite ethnic group, how their resources never quite ran out; of dangers averted or overcome, of hope. . . . After three hours, Sam suggested that the congregation might like to go home. "But where do we go?" they replied, and urged him to continue. Eventually we shared the peanuts and people thronged round us to chat.

—From the report of an ecumenical team to eastern Zaire. *The Rwandan Refugee Crisis,* Geneva: World Council of Churches, 1994.

In spite of vigorous efforts over the last two and a half years by the United Nations, the Rwandan government, and the host governments to encourage refugees to return home, the results have been disappointing. Most refugees who fled the violence in 1994—primarily Hutus fearful of Tutsi revenge—did not return in spite of the Rwandan government's promises. Although 1.2 million Rwandans did return, almost all were "old caseload" refugees—mostly Tutsis who had fled earlier rounds of violence in 1959 or 1963. A troubling environmental factor has been that the repatriates frequently bring cattle, thus increasing the stress on Rwanda's already limited land.

But the donor governments were losing interest in Rwanda, and the host governments were growing impatient. There seemed no other way—the refugees had to return home. In November 1996, rebel Tutsi forces mounted a military attack on Goma, forcing the refugees to flee their camps. Most of them took this opportunity to leave for home. Almost 700,000 refugees returned from Zaire in the course of one month. Way stations were hastily set up to provide food and water to those on foot. Many of the Hutu militants who had dominated the camps retreated deeper into Zaire. As the rebel forces began capturing more territory in Zaire, the refugees retreated into ever more inaccessible places.

A month after the Rwandan refugees began returning from Zaire, the Tanzanian government started rounding up refugees and sending them home, whether they wanted to go or not. Unlike in Zaire, this time the return was not so voluntary. In fact, when UNHCR protested that refugees should not be forced back at gunpoint, the Tanzanian government made clear that it was in charge. UNHCR had no choice but to go along with a less than voluntary situation.

The Rwandan government is trying to deal simultaneously with the massive tasks of absorbing more than 2 million returnees and beginning the process of reconstruction. Violence has escalated in rural parts of the country, and providing humanitarian relief is very difficult. It is not safe for relief workers or human rights monitors to travel in large parts of the country. Progress in charging the perpetrators of the genocide has been painfully slow. Although there are many examples of Hutus and Tutsis getting along, reconciliation remains a distant goal. The situation continues to be volatile; popular demands for justice—and for vengeance—are strong. The situations in neighboring Burundi and Zaire are also deeply troubling.

Genevieve Jacques, a specialist in international affairs for the World Council of Churches, visited Rwanda in March 1997 and reported that Rwanda "is currently under heavy pressure from the international community for hasty reconciliation and quick forgiveness. This is deeply hurting those who had loved ones killed in the genocide which swept the country in 1994. Today is still a time of heavy silence between the Rwandans. External pressure for reconciliation and forgiveness shows a complete lack of understanding that it is only three years since the genocide and that this was the result of a deep and long-standing ideology based on ethnic division. "Today everybody is doing reconciliation!" complains Jacques. "Just as the whole world came to Rwanda with humanitarian aid after the genocide, now there is a huge influx of people coming to 'do reconciliation.'" Jacques herself met one independent missionary from the USA who had come to "reconcile the Rwandans"! He did not speak French or the local language. . . . However, Jacques is also critical of mainstream churches and the worldwide ecumenical family. Previously there were 12 Protestant denominations in Rwanda; now there are 48. The fragmentation in Rwanda is a reflection of our own ecumenical fragmentation and it does not help.

—From World Council of Churches press release, 13 March 1997.

Lessons from Rwanda

1. The causes of the violence in Rwanda are many. Ethnic tension is a product of Rwanda's history and, particularly, of the policies of colonial powers. But ethnic tension was exacerbated by shortages of land, overpopulation, economic disparities, political manipulation—and the pressure of refugees in neighboring countries. If those Rwandans displaced by earlier rounds of violence had been living in peace and security at home, they would not have formed armies and invaded Rwanda—an action that precipitated the hardening of positions.

2. The media are a powerful force. Their role—particularly the radio stations controlled by extremist political parties and paramilitary groups—in stirring up frenzy and hysteria cannot be overlooked. People were constantly told that they would be annihilated unless they acted first—by killing their neighbors before their neighbors killed them.

3. Early warning does not necessarily mean early action by the international community. The signs of tension and the likelihood of widespread violence were all evident by 1993. The UN Security Council could have imposed an arms embargo on Rwanda and expanded the mandate of UNAMIR to include monitoring of human rights abuses and arms acquisitions. Lack of effective leadership by the Security Council, especially by its permanent members, meant that many people died.

> We must all recognize that . . . we have failed in our response to the agony of Rwanda, and thus have acquiesced in the continued loss of human lives. Our readiness and our capacity for action has been demonstrated to be inadequate at best, and deplorable at worst, owing to the absence of collective political will.
> —Boutros Boutros-Ghali. From *Report of the Secretary-General on the Situation in Rwanda,* 31 May 1994, New York: United Nations.

4. The economic, environmental, and political cost to Rwanda's neighbors of taking in the refugees for more than two years was substantial. It has contributed to instability in the region—and to a backlash against the presence of refugees. If renewed conflict in Rwanda, Burundi, or Zaire were to uproot large numbers of people, it would be difficult for them to find protection or welcome in neighboring countries.

5. The return of the Rwandan refugees was largely the result of pressure from the host governments, coupled in the case of Zaire by flight of the militant Hutu leaders from the camps. The importance of separating armed factions from civilian refugees cannot be overemphasized. It is extremely difficult for UN officials on site to refuse armed fighters entry to the refugee camps. However, when the camps are controlled by extremists, refugee assistance and return become much more difficult. Some agencies wonder to what extent their food aid was used by extremists to purchase additional arms, thus pro-longing the suffering.

6. The international community has a chance to learn from its failures in Rwanda. As violence heats up in Burundi—for the same constellation of reasons that led to genocide in Rwanda—there are some signs that we are learning from our mistakes. African governments are imposing their own arms embargo and economic sanctions. They are moving to close their borders to Burundi, ostensibly as a way of pressuring the political leaders to resolve their differences without violence, but also to ensure that Burundian refugees do not pour into their territory. There are fewer signs of hope in the former Zaire (now the Democratic Republic of Congo), where rebel forces at the time of this writing have taken control of the country.

Rwanda is a terrible story—a tale of tragedy, atrocities, hatred, and fear. This account has emphasized the tragic aspects of the violence, but there are also many stories of courageous actions by individuals—of Hutus who hid Tutsis from rampaging gangs, and of Hutus and Tutsis who are today sharing houses until they can build new ones together. Too often such individuals paid for their compassion with their lives. The uncertainty facing Rwanda and neighboring Burundi and Zaire makes it difficult to predict what will happen. The underlying causes for the violence still exist: land is insufficient, environmental degradation is worsening, and suspicion and hatred between ethnic groups remains high. The political will and compassion of the international community is waning.

While the future for Rwanda appears unsettled, it is important to remember that just a few years ago most observers saw the situation in Mozambique as equally hopeless. Mozambique had suffered a sixteen-year-old war, its civilian population had been subjected to brutal atrocities, and the country was littered with land-mines. Two million refugees lived in neighboring countries; another million lived as internally displaced people. The Mozambican economy was shattered, its political institutions discredited, and its people demoralized. But in the space of two short years a peace agreement was signed, UN peacekeeping forces were deployed, elections were held, a new government was installed, and the refugees returned home. Although peace in Mozambique is fragile, although the process of rebuilding will be arduous, and although the country is desperately poor, Mozambique offers hope that long and bitter wars can be ended and that people can rebuild and recover. Mozambique offers hope to Rwanda.

The world's uprooted

have a thousand different faces, a thousand different kinds of experience—but one thing in common: Their homes, sense of stability, regular work, network of family and friends have been disrupted—often brutally, often forever. Beyond all else, that central fact remains.

In the following pages we catch a glimpse of those faces. Vietnamese "boat people"—desperate human beings who fled for their lives. Infinitely sad children of Rwanda—orphans in the midst of unimaginable chaos. But, as well, Indochinese children at work in an orderly school setting. And—also at work—a Laotian silversmith and a Somalian maker of soap, focused and responsible in the midst of the potentially crippling uncertainty and boredom of their refugee camps.

There is also concern and caring—and cleanliness and medical attention in the midst of squalor: a Rwandan nurse attending the sick and dying in Goma's cholera epidemic.

Sometimes there is even fun, to judge by the broad smile on a young Guatemalan guitarist as he waits for resettlement transport. And there is fun at the birthday party of a small and solemn Bosnian refugee, celebrating with her new American friends.

But the sense of bewilderment, hurt, and anger is deep—especially with older persons who have lost everything: family, home, friends—and, beyond even that, such intangibles as satisfying careers, records of personal achievement, all the components of lives well and responsibly lived. It is a pain all too evident in the faces and body language of displaced Croatians, caught up in the terror and brutality of events in the former Yugoslavia.

As Christians, we need to know that these things are happening to our sisters and brothers. We dare not avert our eyes from things that seem too hard to bear. We are not bearing them. They are. We dare not lose our humanity nor our response as children of God to the needs of millions of God's family—our family.

Above: Guatemalan children, part of group accepting voluntary resettlement, wait for transport back home from Mexico.

Below: In Zagreb, Croatia, children of refugees from Vukovar are under care of United Nations Protection Force.

Vietnamese boat people are rescued in South China Sea.

Rwandan refugees forced to leave Goma, Zaire, because of cholera epidemic, struggle to survive in camp outside city.

59

Rwandan refugees are resettled in camps outside Goma because of epidemic.

Rwandan nurse cares for cholera victim near Goma.

Young Rwandan children cry for their mothers at Ndosha camp in Goma, where many, young and old, died of cholera.

Displaced Croatian woman waits to be transferred from shelter in Serb-occupied Croatia to one in Croatian-held territory.

UN Photo 186208/M. Grafman, Doc. 10446

Displaced ethnic Croatians prepare to leave school where they found temporary shelter.

Above: Guatemalan children attend school in Mexico.

Below: Student is hard at work in language class for resettled Indochinese refugees in Sweden.

Above: Silversmith practices his craft in Chiang Kham camp for Laotian hill tribe refugees.

Below: Ethiopian woman makes soap in Jalalaqsi refugee camp, Somalia.

American Baptist National Ministries

Derrill Bazzy

Above: Hannadi Agic, refugee child from Bosnia, celebrates second birthday with children of Calvary Baptist Church, Towson, Maryland.

Below: Young Nicaraguan expatriates awaiting transport, pass time in temporary shelters.

FOUR

Two Nations of Immigrants

In the well-known passage from Matthew 25, we are told that when we minister to the stranger, we are serving Jesus Christ: "When did I see you as a stranger, Lord?" Paradoxically, even as modern communications bring the world into our living rooms and as our children scoop up the latest news on the Internet, it is becoming harder to respond to the stranger among us. Sometimes it may be easier to respond to uprooted people in places like Rwanda than to those living in our own countries.

The Bible is filled with stories about the transforming power of encounters with strangers. Christ himself sought out strangers, approached them, talked with them—and, in so doing, challenged the prevailing code of behavior. In John 4, we are presented with the radical story of Jesus' encounter with a Samaritan woman at a well. The Samaritans lived lives separate from the Jews (as the scriptures say, "Jews do not share things in common with Samaritans"), and this woman with her history of five husbands must surely have been a social outcast. But Jesus not only reached out to her, he revealed himself as the Messiah, and she, in turn, spread the good news in her community.

In today's United States and Canada, the closest modern counterpart to the biblical Samaritans is likely to be immigrant groups that differ from the dominant culture. Both nations are increasingly diverse, with immigrants from many different parts of the world. Too often, however, we stay with our own kind, don't seek out the strangers among us, don't ask questions of the Korean greengrocer or the Mexican working in the meatpacking plant. Sometimes we don't even *see* them. While both Canada and the United States are proud of their immigrant heritage, backlash against the immigrants arriving now is very real. It has become politically acceptable for the politicians of a receiver nation to blame new immigrants for that nation's failure to provide for the economic and social well-being of its own people. It is easier to blame immigrants for urban unemployment than to address the structural causes that prevent increasing numbers of citizens from finding jobs that enable them to live in security and dignity. But it is much harder to blame or scapegoat immigrants once you learn to know them.

Nations of Immigrants

Unlike most nations in the world, Canada and the United States have traditionally been countries of immigration. They have prided themselves on their heritage as places of refuge for those fleeing political and religious persecution or poverty. However, it must be stated that this heritage—nations of immigrants, havens for the persecuted, melting pots or salad bowls— has never met the ideal. Immigrants have not always been well treated, and—to the shame of both nations—North America as haven for European refugees was achieved at immeasurable cost to indigenous cultures.

There have been earlier periods of persecution and discrimination against immigrants: the Chinese in the latter part of the 1800s, Irish and Italians in the early part of this century, and citizens of Japanese origin during World War II. Throughout the 1980s and continuing into the 1990s, the backlash has been against Asians and undocumented Mexican, African, and other visibly different immigrants—different, that is, from the Caucasian majority. Historically, the backlash paralleled economic trends. When economic conditions were good and there was a need for labor, the two governments adopted more welcoming policies.

When times were tough, there was a tendency to blame foreigners for domestic problems and clamp down on immigration. But the economic connection does not explain the full extent of the present resistance. People also fear the encroachment of other cultures, languages, and religions. Furthermore, the current backlash against immigration surely reflects the fact that in both the United States and Canada, European immigrants have been largely replaced by those from Asia, Latin America, and, to a much lesser extent, Africa.

But their understanding of themselves as havens for the world's persecuted has been at the heart of the two nations' identities from the very beginning (with the significant exceptions of both countries' treatment of their native peoples, and of the United States' appalling embrace of slavery). Most Canadian and U.S. citizens can trace their ancestry back to immigrants or refugees—some a generation or two, some much further back. This reality has shaped the political cultures and institutions of the two countries. In both the United States and Canada, for example, ethnic lobbies have been important political actors.

This heritage sets us apart from most other countries. In Germany, for example, citizenship is determined by one's ancestry. You are German if your ancestors were German, even if they settled in the Ukraine four hundred years ago, even if you speak no German. You are considered German if you have German blood. Similarly, some years ago Japan (which has one of the most restrictive immigration policies in the world) announced that people of Japanese ancestry could return "home." Several thousand Brazilian and Peruvian citizens whose ancestors had migrated from Japan in previous centuries took advantage of the offer and went to Japan. They spoke no Japanese, and their cultural upbringing had been Latin American for generations. Yet the Japanese considered them to be Japanese. At the same time, the Japanese refuse to allow Koreans who have lived in Japan for generations to become Japanese citizens.

Sometimes in North America we focus so much on our inadequacies in remaining true to this heritage as countries of immigration, that we forget how revolutionary a concept it was—and still is. The belief that people of many different nationalities, religions, and ethnic origins can not only become Canadian or United States citizens, but may reach the highest levels of political and economic power in their adopted countries remains a powerful symbol—and a beacon.

> I'm an Iranian refugee and have been living in Sweden for six years. I speak Swedish and have a good job. The government has been very good to us and people are helpful. But I want to go to the United States. I know life will be more difficult for me there—there's a lot of discrimination against Muslims and there is no government health care like we have here. But in the United States, I have a chance to become an American and to be treated as an American. Here I can become a Swedish citizen, but the Swedes will never see me as a real Swede. Even my children will always be seen as different, as foreigners.
>
> —Iranian refugee, Uppsala, Sweden. From an interview with the author, 1993.

Although this chapter deals with both Canada and the United States, the two countries are different in important respects, particularly their policies toward refugees. Throughout most of the past fifty years, U.S. refugee policies have been dominated by the Cold War; approximately 95 percent of refugees admitted to the United States between 1945 and 1989 were from communist countries, that is, designated enemy governments. Although the Canadian government was clearly aligned with the West during the Cold War, its refugee policy was less politicized. In 1974, for example, in the aftermath of the Chilean coup against socialist president Salvador Allende, Canada opened its doors to some seven thousand Chilean refugees. Only a handful were admitted to the United States. (And, given U.S. involvement in Chilean politics, most Chilean refugees did not want to come to the United States.) To some degree this reflects Canada's long-standing commitment to multilateral institutions, particularly the United Nations, and its commitment to international law. As a superpower, the United States became accustomed to taking actions perceived to be in its national interest, whether or not they were consistent with international standards. Canada—like other mid-sized Western powers—realized that its national interests lay with the creation of strong multilateral institutions and the rule of law.

Although the Cold War is over, political interests continue to influence U.S. policy toward refugees. This is manifest today in the different approaches taken by Canada and the United States toward human rights issues in China and to Chinese asylum-seekers. In the United States, conservative forces, including fundamentalist Christian groups, have allied themselves with members of Congress in advocating refugee status for Chinese fleeing their country because of the one-child policy and forced abortion. While forcing a woman to have an abortion is clearly a violation of her human rights, both governments are fearful that large numbers of Chinese will come to pursue asylum claims on those grounds. The Clinton administration has opposed the granting of asylum to individuals claiming to flee the forced abortion policy, arguing that all Chinese are subject to the one-child policy and that individuals have not been singled out for persecution. The new immigration legislation, adopted in 1996, contains a curious provision which accepts opposition to the one-child policy as grounds for refugee status, but limits the number of refugee claims on that basis to one thousand people.

Canadian immigration policies in the post-Cold War era appear to be shaped by three concerns: (1) to attract "good quality" immigrants through its refugee program in order to continue its task of nation-building; (2) to maintain control over immigration—by not appearing so attractive that all the world's refugees will come; and (3) to maintain a posture seen as "liberal" in order to support Canada's disproportionate international diplomatic role in the Western alliance.

In Canada and the United States, the emphasis is on family immigration. The principle that immigrant citizens or residents should be able to reunite with family members still living abroad has been a bedrock of both countries' immigration policies. Another principle of immigration policy shared by the United States and Canada is the need to admit skilled workers to meet labor needs. Both countries have systems in place that give priority to immigration of skilled workers in occupations with a labor shortage. Thus, it is easier for a trained health professional or athlete to immigrate than for a lawyer or secretary. Both countries also have special "fast-track" programs enabling persons with substantial funds to emigrate if they intend to invest a certain amount of money in the national economy. Canadian policy appears to be shifting toward more emphasis on business immigration and a corresponding decrease in family immigration. An important principle of immigration policy in both countries is that refugees be admitted as a humanitarian response to need. While both countries have admitted refugees in accord with political attitudes prevailing at a given time, U.S. policies toward refugee admissions have been much more politically motivated than those of Canada. Internationally, Canada has a reputation for having a "kinder, gentler" approach to refugees than the United States—a reputation that, as we shall see, is mostly well founded.

All together, the United States receives about 800,000 legal immigrants a year. Of these, two-thirds come to reunite with families, approximately 100,000 come as refugees, and the rest come for employment. In Canada, some 200,000 immigrants come every year, of whom about a third come as family members, about a third as refugees or asylum-seekers, and the rest for employment.

While there are strong feelings in both countries against illegal immigration, it is presently a "hotter" political issue in the United States than in Canada. This is because of the greater numbers of undocumented migrants in the United States (currently estimated at 300,000 per year) and the concentration of undocumented migrants in a few politically important states.

In the past several years, public opinion polls have shown that a majority of Americans think illegal immigration is a serious problem and should be restricted. (The polls also show considerable confusion about legal versus undocumented immigration.) Much of the anger and fear behind U.S. public concern with undocumented migrants is directed toward Mexican and Central American immigrants and focuses on the southern border—the three thousand miles dividing Mexico and the United States is the longest border in the world between a developing and a developed country. Conversely, there is little public outcry in the United States about the estimated 50 percent of illegal immigrants from countries such as Ireland, Italy, and Canada, who overstay their visas. The Canadian government, not surprisingly, has traditionally seen issues of Mexican and Central American immigration as largely U.S. problems. This was particularly so in the early 1980s when U.S. involvement in Central America was highly politicized.

In November 1994, Californians approved Proposition 187 with 59 percent of the vote, thereby instructing public employees to deny public health, education, and social services to undocumented immigrants, or, more ominously, to people "suspected" of being illegal immigrants. Implementation of Proposition 187 has been halted in the courts, but its effects are clearly apparent. Racism against people who look "foreign" or whose skin is darker or who speak with a foreign accent is growing, as manifested, for example, by the refusal of bus drivers to allow people who "look" Latino or Asian to board their buses, or when pregnant women are afraid to seek medical help for fear of deportation. As a result of the campaign around Proposition 187, immigrants are being portrayed as a burden. Furthermore, its passage had a galvanizing effect on politicians throughout the country when they realized there was political capital to be made on this issue. However, efforts to replicate Proposition 187 in other states and on the federal level have so far been unsuccessful.

So then you are no longer strangers and aliens, but you are citizens with the saints and also members of the household of God. Eph. 2:19.

Another manifestation of the backlash against immigrants in the United States is the growing militarization of the southern border. Even as the U.S. Congress cut social programs and emphasized the need to balance the budget, it allocated almost double the resources available for border control, enabling the Immigration and Naturalization Service to fortify the southern border near San Diego and El Paso with additional border patrol agents, flood lights, ten-foot-high steel fences, and more sophisticated computer and tracking technology.

Because of its geography, history, and type of economy, the Canadian approach to curbing illegal immigration has taken a different form. Compared with the United States there is less variety in employment, and immigrants generally do not come to Canada for jobs. As Tom Clark, director of Canada's Inter-Church Committee for Refugees, says, "If you want the American dream, you go to the United States. If you want refuge and you're from a Commonwealth country, you'll aim for the United Kingdom, Australia, or Canada." The Canadian government has imposed visa restrictions to keep people, particularly those from troubled countries, from coming to Canada. Furthermore, Canada is concerned about people crossing its border with the United States.

Thus, the Canadian government has been the driving force behind efforts to work out an arrangement with the U.S. government to reduce the number of people coming through the United States to Canada.

In the long public debates over the North American Free Trade Agreement (NAFTA), remarkably little overt attention was paid to issues of migration. The agreement itself includes minimal provisions concerning migration, affecting only a small number of commercial travelers. But NAFTA could have major consequences on Mexican migration to the United States. In the short run, it may actually act as a stimulus, although its supporters argue that if NAFTA leads to higher economic growth for Mexico, migration will eventually decline. In the meanwhile, we need to consider migration when we debate trade policies. We have accepted global markets, but not global migration; we have legitimized and extolled free trade while denying free movement of people.

> When Westerners come to our countries to work, they are called "expatriate experts." When we come to their countries with our diplomas, we become "migrant workers."
>
> —Colombian lawyer and former judge exiled in Rome. *A Moment to Choose: Risking to Be with Uprooted People, A Resource Book.* Geneva: World Council of Churches, 1997.

Refugee Resettlement

In both the United States and Canada, refugee resettlement programs were developed in the years immediately after World War II. Both countries saw themselves as places for permanent resettlement, not merely temporary havens from which people could be repatriated after stability in their homeland was restored. National legislation was developed and large bureaucracies were created to process refugees for admission and assist them in adapting to North American life. In both countries, refugee resettlement policy was based on the understanding that refugees would be selected by government officials "over there" and would come to North America in an orderly, managed fashion. Among other things, those selected for resettlement would be given language training and cultural orientation before leaving the camps in countries of first asylum.

Canada

In Canada, refugees are admitted to the country through two programs. Government-assisted refugees are selected by the Canadian government overseas and assisted with resettlement in Canada. A private-sponsorship program enables private groups (including churches) to identify specific refugees to be resettled by those groups. But, even for privately sponsored refugees, it is always the government that determines whether or not a particular refugee can be admitted. In fact, the number of both government-assisted and privately sponsored refugees admitted to Canada has been declining. From 1988–90, an average of 13,400 refugees per year came to Canada through the government-assisted program; from 1991–93, the number fell to approximately 6,800. Private sponsorship has fallen even more precipitously, from 21,631 in 1989 to 4,737 in 1993. This is because the process is slow and because the government rejects many cases identified by private groups. It is really hard, for example, when a church is all fired up to resettle a particular refugee, waits for one or two years, and then finds that the case is rejected by the Canadian government.

Unlike the United States, the Canadian government applies two criteria for allowing refugees to enter the country. First, an individual must be found to fit the definition of refugee under Canadian law. If she or he is found eligible, a second set of standards kicks in: will the refugee, with help, if necessary, become a contributing member of Canadian society? Thus, the government looks at an individual's background, education, occupational skills, and skills in the official language(s) to determine whether he or she—already classified as a refugee—will be allowed to enter the country. This means that there are many very needy people without a basic education or French/English language skills who will not be admitted to Canada as refugees.

Once the individual has been judged eligible and admissible, security checks and medical exams are carried out and the refugee travels to Canada. The refugee receives a loan from the government to pay for his or her travel. Once in Canada—whether through overseas processing or by applying for refugee status in Canada—the individual must be "landed." This means receiving permission to enter or remain in Canada in order to establish permanent residence. Overall, both the number of refugees and that of refugees as a percentage of all immigrants have been declining. In 1989, 37,389 refugees—or 19.4 percent of all immigrants to Canada that year—were "landed." By 1994, the figure had dropped to 17,479—less than half the number of five years earlier—only 7.9 percent of all immigrant landings. The reduced number is a result of diminishing resources for government-sponsored overseas refugee resettlement, the high rejection rate for privately sponsored refugees, and administrative barriers such as the landing fee, or "head tax."

The decline in immigration has emerged as a controversial issue in Canada. In February 1995, the government imposed a $975 "Right of Landing Fee" on each adult refugee or immigrant being "landed." This applies to those selected overseas (government and private) as well as to asylum-seekers recognized as refugees (who must also pay a $500 processing fee). For both types of refugee this represents a tremendous burden. Recent arrivals rarely have the money to pay these fees in order to bring their families into Canada from refugee camps in other parts of the world. Imposing a tax on family reunification (in addition, of course, to the loans taken out to pay for transportation to Canada) is a long way from the North American heritage as a place of refuge for the world's persecuted.

Once an individual refugee or a refugee family is accepted into and arrives in Canada, the process of adjusting to life in a new country begins. In Canada, as in the United States, community and church involvement have both been essential for the successful adaptation of refugees. Through a variety of sponsorship programs, individual refugees are welcomed to the country and receive the necessary support to find employment and housing, to enroll children in school, and to learn about life in the new world. At a time when much ecumenical refugee work is being handed over to specialized agencies, the local congregational involvement in refugee resettlement in these countries is striking. In both Canada and the United States, the growth of ethnic-specific organizations by former refugees has been an important source of immediate and long-term support for new arrivals.

But the process of adapting to life in another country—particularly one with a different climate, unfamiliar customs, and a new language—is difficult. Overall, the record of resettlement in Canada and the United States has been very positive; people from very different backgrounds have been enabled to begin new lives. There are, however, differences in adjustment between ethnic groups. Hmong refugees in the United States, for example, have experienced particular difficulties in becoming self-sufficient, while Somali refugees in Canada have adapted quickly. There are also generational differences. Older people, particularly those who have lost many family members to violence, generally have a more difficult time than children in making the transition. Uneven patterns of adjustment may place strains on family life. A common phenomenon is that children embrace the new culture and reject efforts by their parents to raise them in the traditional norms of their former home.

On the night of April 29th, 1975, I was on a barge packed with refugees, floating down the Saigon River trying to reach international waters. Fierce fighting was going on, on both sides of the river, and the sky was red with fire. By early morning we had reached the Pacific Ocean and heard over a portable radio that the communists had taken control of South Vietnam. I could still see the coast of my homeland but it was not mine anymore. I did not cry and I was not afraid. Fear is when airplanes fly over your neighborhood and your body shakes uncontrollably and the next bomb could be on your house. . . . The first time I cried was a week later in a refugee camp in Guam. . . .

My first year in Montreal, Canada, was mostly spent on survival. There was no time for deep thinking or feelings. My father, who had been a successful businessman in Vietnam, discovered he could not even get a job as a bookkeeper. My mother, who ran the complex family business, could not even get a driving license due to the language barrier. I speak English and French, had an American university degree, but could not even get a job as a bank teller or cashier at the supermarket. I finally got my first job as a receptionist at a small company two hours away from the city. My brothers and sisters delivered pizza at night in the Canadian winter with light jackets, no boots, and a cheap unreliable car. We felt like we were always swimming underwater. Yet every night, we counted our blessings. We were all alive and the family was intact.

It was only by the third year that we started to feel alive. . . . For the first time since I had escaped Vietnam, I had time to wonder about my future. "Is this how I wanted to spend my life? Where did I want to go, where did I want to be in ten years?" Somehow all the answers were: "Back home. . . ."

> When does a refugee stop being a refugee? I stopped being a refugee the day I took back control of my life. The guilt will always be there, every day, and worst on holidays when I wonder, why me, what makes me so different that I am here in this comfortable life and not rotting at the bottom of the ocean or in a refugee camp? The nightmares will always be there. But I thank God every day for giving me this second chance.
>
> —From "A Refugee Story" by Xuan Nguyen Sutter, *Women's Commission News,* Women's Commission for Refugee Women and Children, International Rescue Committee, New York, February 1994.

United States

Although Americans are justifiably proud of their large-scale resettlement programs, admission of refugees has always been shaped by foreign policy concerns. In 1980, the United States government passed a new refugee law which eliminated the legal basis for preference to victims of communism. However, the process is designed to give priority to "groups of special humanitarian concern" to the United States government. Thus, by the mid-1990s most refugees admitted to the United States were from the former Soviet Union (primarily Jewish) and from Indochina (primarily Vietnamese).

In a unique departure from internationally accepted practice, most refugees who come to the United States are not refugees in the normal sense because they apply for resettlement while they are still in their country of origin. This procedure, known as in-country processing, was initially developed in Vietnam to insure the survival of more refugees, many of whom were dying. Rather than subject them to the danger of their small treacherous boats, the reasoning went, they could be processed directly from Vietnam. This procedure, known as the Orderly Departure Program, became a huge undertaking employing hundreds of staff to process Vietnamese for admission to the United States. Similarly in the former Soviet Union, individuals are accepted as refugees for resettlement in the United States while still in their home country. Currently, more than 80 percent of refugees admitted to the United States come directly from their home countries through these in-country programs.

While the U.S. government is undoubtedly right that lives are being saved by eliminating the dangers of refugee flight, it creates a very curious situation. By definition, refugees are persons who fear persecution from their governments; but in order to operate these in-country programs the United States must negotiate directly with the "persecuting" government. Furthermore, there are situations in which refugees are not allowed to leave the country—even though judged to be refugees by the U.S. government—because their own government refuses to give them permission to leave!

The United States sets an overall ceiling as well as regional ceilings for refugee admissions. The overall ceiling has been declining precipitously—from 130,000 in fiscal year 1994 to 75,000 in fiscal 1997. Since the regional ceilings are still too low to meet the regions' needs—there are, for example, only seven thousand admission slots for Africa—the State Department sets up processing priorities. Currently, top priority is given (in descending order) to cases in urgent need of protection referred by UNHCR; cases of particular interest to the U.S. government (for example, political prisoners from Cuba); and refugees with family ties in the United States. It is a complex system. Once individuals are identified as eligible and prescreened, an official from the Immigration and Naturalization Service (INS) actually decides whether or not they will be admitted.

Unlike the Canadian system, the United States government uses no criteria to determine how well refugees seeking admittance are likely to adapt to the United States (except for the exclusion of certain classes of criminals). The U.S. program, for all its shortcomings, is still primarily intended to rescue people in need of protection. As does Canada, the United States government lends money to an accepted refugee for the purchase of airline tickets. Once the refugee has arrived in the United States, voluntary agencies, including Church World Service (CWS), provide that individual with services through congregations and affiliated offices throughout the country.

In both Canada and the United States, resettlement processing is time-consuming and cumbersome. Individuals who have fled for their lives must wait many months in a refugee camp while paperwork flies back and forth. A short interview with an INS official or a Canadian visa officer—sometimes lasting twenty minutes, at most an hour—determines whether an individual will be resettled, remain in a refugee camp, or be repatriated.

Beyond their cumbersome nature, however, these procedures raise some serious ethical issues. We know that all the world's refugees cannot come to the United States or Canada. But among the world's 27 million or so refugees, who should be given the opportunity? Church partners in Africa, for example, accuse resettlement governments of "skimming off" the elite and taking the potential leaders and educated classes of refugees from the continent. This accusation rings particularly true of Canada, which has admissions policies that explicitly include criteria related to education, language, and skills. But it is also true of the United States, because well-educated refugees are more likely to be able to prove that they have been singled out for persecution rather than simply caught in the cross fire of a civil war.

There are other difficult questions as well. The original intent of resettlement was to move people whose lives were in danger, for example, refugees who were being threatened by political groups in the camp. But the substantial pressure from refugees already resettled in the United States and Canada to bring in their relatives creates the need for complex decisions: what, for example, is more important—to bring in the mother of adult refugees who miss her, or a person who is living somewhere under a death threat? While you can make a good argument for the protection case, in practice it is really tough to tell the refugee in your office or congregation that his or her mother is not a priority and that other refugees are in greater need of resettlement.

Resettlement brings up a host of other issues as refugees struggle to adapt to life in North America. Churches have traditionally done wonderful work in welcoming refugees to their communities, helping them to learn English, and advocating on their behalf with various authorities. But to what extent should refugees be encouraged to maintain their own culture and language? Does a church sponsor have the right or the responsibility to challenge racist attitudes held by refugees, or to discourage refugees from sending money to armed factions in their former home?

There are also questions of particular concern to churches. Most churches are careful to respect the religious beliefs of the refugees they assist in resettlement, but some regard them as a fertile mission field. This puts the refugees into a vulnerable position:

they may find it difficult to say no to these nice church people. They may also be going through some spiritual uncertainty as a result of their experience. Ironically, the churches that have been most careful to respect the religious traditions of refugees they resettle are much less ethnically diverse today than those that have seen refugees as potential new members. But, in many cases, ministry to refugees provides a unique opportunity to engage in levels of mutual understanding that transcend the boundaries of a particular faith perspective.

When Osman [a Bosnian Muslim refugee resettled by my church in Fredericksburg, Virginia] came, I found out not only did he have a heart problem, he also had cancer. I took him to the doctor, and I was his confidant. We spoke, and we spent much time talking about dying. "What a gift, a man brought his family to freedom, and they were safe with people who cared in America! That's what you provide," he said, tears streaming from his eyes.

When we went to the cancer doctor, he said "There's nothing we can do. Whatever he wants to do. . . ." We walked out of there. . . . Was it a time to be sad? I was sorry that he wasn't going to have longer. I said, "Let's go to the beach." He had told me how much he loved the beach when he was at home and life was good. So the whole family went down to Virginia Beach, and we had a wonderful time. We ate. We walked. And Osman, who had lost seventy five pounds, even got his son's trunks on and went into the water. He lay on the beach with his wife so he would have wonderful memories, and when the time came, I held his hand.

We had talked much about death. We had talked much about God taking us and how wonderful it was that he had this opportunity to see his family happy. His son was in school, and he had started working. His wife had food to cook, and life was not so difficult.

As his wife stood on one side holding his hand and I stood on the other side holding his hand, we told him, she being Muslim, I being Christian, that our God was going to be with him, and he left.

I gave a little talk at the funeral. There were two funerals, one Muslim, one Christian. He was a "Methodist Muslim," and he told everyone that. On Friday nights he went to be with his Muslim friends and on Sundays he came to be with his Methodist friends because, you see, all God's people were with him together.

—Barbara Gear, First United Methodist Church, Fredericksburg, Virginia.

After we had been refugees in Croatia for a year and a half, my father found out about an organization that helps people come to America. We decided to try it because it wasn't easy living in Croatia. We had interviews and then were allowed to come here.

I like America because people here can say what they think and most other people will respect that, even though maybe they don't agree with another's opinion. Here, almost no one asks what nationality you are, and I like that. All that matters is that you be a good person and try to help others. On the other hand, I don't like America because of the big contrast between people, between the rich ones and the homeless ones.

School here is much easier than in Bosnia. The tests are not difficult and there are no oral examinations. Students don't respect the teachers enough and they don't behave well. They eat and drink during class periods and some of the teachers do the same. It shouldn't be like that, because discipline is very important. Students here also don't know much about the rest of the world. They only know about America and about nothing else.

I really miss my country and I often think about it. But if somebody asked me if I want to go back, I would say no. Bosnia isn't the same anymore. It's completely destroyed and there is so much hatred between people in it. I just hope that one day every-thing will be normal again and that the people will again have the chance for a decent life, because everybody in this world has a right to that.

—Ajila Potur, 14-year-old Bosnian refugee student, California. From Women's Commission for Refugee Women and Children, International Rescue Committee, New York, 1994.

Responding to Strangers on the Border

Although resettlement procedures and policies were already well established in the United States and Canada, these policies were challenged in the mid-1980s by the dramatic increase in people arriving directly on the countries' borders. Neither nation had much experience with this situation. The United States had traditionally dealt with Mexican and Central American labor-driven immigration, but with the exception of the Cuban influx of the mid-1960s, few people had arrived on the nations' shores and airports claiming that their lives would be in danger if they were sent back.

Both Canadian and U.S. refugee policies were based on the premise that the governments would select deserving refugees "over there" and that their migration to North America would be orderly and controlled. Although both countries were prepared for the occasional asylum-seeker who turned up on the border, the systems were not equipped to handle thousands—or, in the case of the United States, hundreds of thousands—of refugees who suddenly arrived on the border or in airports asking for asylum.

Canada

In Canada, the number of asylum-seekers jumped from approximately five thousand in 1984 to thirty thousand in 1988, straining the system and putting increased pressure on the government. Canadian procedures were unable to keep up with this pace, and the backlog of cases mounted. In 1989, new refugee-determination procedures were introduced to speed up the process. But the government still faced a huge backlog of pending cases from the old system. For individual asylum-seekers, the years of limbo while decisions were made about their refugee claims were often unbearable. In late 1990, the Inter-Church Committee for Refugees (ICCR) submitted a report to the United Nations Human Rights Commission charging that this accumulation of unresolved cases constituted cruelty to asylum-seekers who had, in some cases, spent years waiting for a decision. In 1991, the ICCR began a campaign to challenge the new refugee laws in the Supreme Court. Although the court eventually decided not to hear the case, the ICCR's challenge marked a turning point in the Canadian churches' growing advocacy on behalf of refugees.

Since then, the number of refugee claims in Canada has decreased, with only 22,000 filed in 1994. Although new procedures have speeded up the processing of current asylum-seekers, the backlog remains. Furthermore, advocates for refugees argue that in speeding up the process, certain safeguards—such as a meaningful appeal procedure—were lost.

Canadian law gives officials very broad "discretionary" powers, but asylum-seekers are granted only limited access to courts. For example, persons can be blocked from a refugee hearing if an official has reasonable grounds to believe that they pose a security risk. The official's decision is hard to challenge. On the other hand, a person can be declared a permanent resident at the border if an official believes such a declaration would not be contrary to the Immigration Act and Regulations. Canadian officials are compelled to make decisions based on imprecise criteria and need not give reasons for their decisions.

In spite of its shortcomings, the Canadian asylum process has many advantages over the U.S. system. In Canada, government-funded legal aid is provided for most refugee claimants to help them prepare for their interviews. In the United States there is no such assistance. Asylum-seekers must garner the necessary resources to hire an attorney on their own, find a pro bono lawyer, or take their chances without legal representation. And the record in the United States is that applicants with legal counsel generally do much better. There are also significant differences in acceptance rates between the two countries. In Canada approximately 70 percent of refugee cases are approved; in the United States the latest figures are about 20 percent. This difference may reflect the fact that the reasons for seeking asylum in Canada and the United States are often very different, and that government decision-making is not based on the same criteria.

In Canada, people waiting to have their cases heard are generally allowed to work as long as nine months, with the possibility of extension. In the United States they are not allowed to work for the first six months, although current policy requires that most cases be decided within that six-month period. In Canada they are eligible for social benefits; in the United States they are not, except for emergency medical treatment. The main groups of asylum-seekers in Canada are Sri Lankans, Iranians, Somalis, and Indians. In the United States they are Central Americans, Mexicans, Chinese, Indians, and Haitians.

Canada has been a leader in gender-based asylum claims. Back in 1993, the Canadian Immigration Review Board issued guidelines for gender-related persecution. In July 1994, asylum was granted to a Somali woman who feared that her ten-year-old daughter would face female circumcision if they were returned to Somalia. Subsequent decisions were made in favor of a Saudi woman who had chosen not to wear the veil, and of an Ecuadorian woman suffering from spousal abuse, who was being ignored by the local police authorities in Ecuador. In 1995, the United States also issued guidelines on gender-based asylum claims, and in 1996 a negative decision was overturned and asylum granted to a Togolese woman fearing female circumcision if she were returned to her home country.

United States

In the 1980s, the United States experienced a dramatic increase in the number of asylum applications it received, resulting in a backlog of 450,000 pending cases. As in Canada, this caused uncertainty and fear among refugees who spent years in limbo while they waited for their asylum interview. In 1995, the U.S. government issued new asylum regulations that were intended to speed up the process. Under the new law, cases are to be decided within 180 days of being filed. For the most part, the U.S. Immigration and Naturalization Service has managed to meet that deadline for cases filed under the new system. This was made possible by doubling the number of asylum officers and generally increasing the resources put into the process. But it will take many years before the 450,000 cases in the backlog are decided. And there are vast differences in the percentage of approvals from country to country: 87 percent of Bosnians and 86 percent of Somalis, for example, are approved, compared with 7 percent of Guatemalans.

The U.S. government was also pressed to change its policies toward Haitians and Cubans arriving in Florida. From 1981 to 1995, United States policy was relatively clear: Cubans who made it to U.S. shores would be allowed to enter the country, adjust their status to that of permanent resident, and eventually become United States citizens. In contrast, Haitians leaving their country would be picked up by ships of the U.S. Coast Guard in a process known as interdiction, and returned to Haiti. In a mild concession to international law, the Haitians were briefly interviewed on board ship, and those found to have credible reasons to fear persecution back home were allowed to enter the United States to file for political asylum. However, over a period of fourteen years some 28,000 Haitians were interdicted, and a mere twenty-eight were found to have reason to fear for their lives.

After the 1991 coup in Haiti, the flood of Haitian refugees led to a change in U.S. policy. Actually, it led to a whole series of changes, sometimes day by day. The violence and the documented persecution in Haiti were so great that initially Haitians were allowed to enter the United States. When the number of arrivals increased dramatically, this policy was changed. Haitians were to be picked up at sea and taken to Jamaica, where their cases would be heard on board a U.S. ship. That policy was dropped after one month because shipboard procedures were overwhelmed by the number of arrivals. Haitians were taken to the U.S. Naval Air Station in Guantanamo Bay, Cuba, where they were to stay until the political situation in Haiti improved.

The influx of Haitian refugees into Florida—and fear of even greater numbers in the future—put major pressure on the U.S. government to seek a political solution in Haiti. In 1994, the United States led a multinational armed force—consisting largely of U.S. troops—to establish order in the country. Eventually, elections were held in Haiti, President Jean-Bertrand Aristide was restored to power, and the Haitian military leaders were forced into exile. Not surprisingly, many refugees at Guantanamo chose to return to Haiti after Aristide's restoration to power; those who did not, were returned against their will.

Throughout the crisis, Canada did not play a visible role in responding to Haitian refugees. When the United States asked for help in sharing the burden, Canada remained silent despite the inherent logic of immigration to French-speaking Quebec with its established Haitian community and the already existing development aid links between Canada and Haiti. Worse still, Canadian ships participating in the embargo intercepted Haitian boats and passed the Haitians over to U.S. authorities for screening.

In May 1995, perhaps as a result of the growing charges of racism in its unequal treatment of Cubans and Haitians, as well as the increasing numbers of Cubans setting sail for Florida, the U.S. government changed its policy toward Cuban asylum-seekers. From that point on, Cubans leaving their country were to be treated just like the Haitians. They would be picked up at sea and returned to Cuba, with a cursory screening so that those with credible fear of persecution could ask for political asylum in the United States. However, the 33,000 Cubans already living at Guantanamo when this policy change went into effect were permitted to enter the United States.

In 1995, the governments of the United States and Canada began negotiations on a so-called Memorandum of Agreement that, with a few exceptions, requires asylum cases to be heard in the country of first arrival. The framing of the agreement was in response to the reality that fully one-third of Canadian asylum cases first passed through the United States. Canada wanted to reduce the number of asylum-seekers coming to its territory by requiring that such cases be decided by the U.S. government.

In practice, a whole network had been developed to help asylum-seekers rejected by the United States to get into Canada, where they had a much better chance of being allowed to stay. The process that had emerged was that asylum-seekers would approach the Canadian authorities at a U.S.–Canadian border post, ask for asylum, be given preliminary interviews, and then return to the U.S. side to wait until a decision was reached in Canada. Many of these waiting asylum-seekers were assisted by U.S. churches. Eventually, many of them were allowed to enter Canada and resume their lives.

Under the terms of the Memorandum of Agreement, this arrangement would no longer be possible. In early 1996, perhaps as a result of the outcry of U.S. and Canadian churches, negotiations concerning the Memorandum of Agreement were suspended and the project was put on hold. The churches argued strongly that refugees should be able to choose where to seek protection, and that a precondition to such an agreement should be the assurance of substantially similar treatment in each country.

Challenges to Current U.S. and Canadian Policy

For more than fifty years in both Canada and the United States, churches have been in the forefront of ministry to refugees, asylum-seekers (or refugee claimants as they are called in Canada), and immigrants. Congregations have welcomed newcomers to their communities and eased the pain of transition for them. In so doing, the local churches frequently benefited more than the refugees they assisted. From the beginning, the churches have not only provided direct service to individual refugees, but have also been outspoken advocates on the policy issues of the day.

In spite of the close cooperation between churches and the two governments on issues of refugee resettlement, there has always been some tension in the church–government partnership, reflecting different interests and values. Governments generally want to give priority to those refugees who are likely to contribute the most to their adopted societies: the educated, the healthy, and the young. Churches are anxious that resettlement be used to assist the most vulnerable, including the disabled, the elderly, and those most physically at risk in their country of origin. In both countries, the churches have pressed for more inclusive resettlement policies in regular meetings with their governments and through mobilization of their constituencies.

In the last decade, as questions about treatment of asylum-seekers have become more politically charged, the churches have taken increasingly active advocacy positions. In particular, Canada's Inter-Church Committee for Refugees has played a path-breaking role in holding its government accountable to international human rights law. Perhaps paralleling differences in the two governments, the Canadian churches have played important roles in the development of international standards, in monitoring UNHCR Executive Committee decisions, and in working through the UN Human Rights Commission. In the United States, meanwhile, the churches have concentrated on mobilizing the domestic church-based constituency to speak out on policy issues affecting refugees and immigrants.

In part, this difference reflects the contexts within which the churches work. In Canada there is no history of domestic human rights work. ICCR took on this responsibility because it was unable to persuade others to do it. In the United States, there are well-established human rights groups that have been engaged by the churches to take on issues such as the treatment of Haitian refugees and the Canadian–U.S. Memorandum of Agreement.

In both countries, church-based organizations are active participants in broader coalitions of NGOs. In Canada, the Inter-Church Committee for Refugees is made up of ten national church bodies, including Catholic organizations, that work together on refugee issues in association with the Canadian Council of Churches. ICCR is an active participant in the broader coalition of nongovernmental organizations that make up the Canadian Council for Refugees. In the United States, the principal ecumenical body is the Church World Service Immigration and Refugee Program, which is part of the National Council of the Churches of Christ in the USA. Although the CWS program has no Catholic participation, in practice there is substantial collaboration in areas of both refugee service and advocacy.

Other church-based agencies in the United States, such as Episcopal Migration Ministries, Lutheran Immigration and Refugee Service, World Relief (an arm of the National Association of Evangelicals), and the U.S. Catholic Conference, are also active in serving refugees as well as advocating for policy changes. Like their Canadian counterparts, Church World Service and other church-based organizations participate in broader coalitions, principally the umbrella organization InterAction's Committee on Refugee and Migration Affairs (which focuses on refugee issues in the United States and internationally) and the National Immigration Forum (which concentrates on the policy agenda).

Canada and Human Rights Instruments

As Tom Clark, director of ICCR, points out, "There are some dramatic contrasts between the conventional image of Canada and its immigration practices. It is, of course, true that Canada hears a respectable number of asylum cases each year (twenty thousand) and allows most of them to remain on one ground or another. It is in the area of the eight thousand or so annual expulsions that problems arise."

In 1994, the UN Human Rights Committee pronounced Canada's expulsion of a Vietnamese asylum-seeker to the United States to be a violation of the Covenant on Civil and Political Rights—the major UN human rights treaty. The Supreme Court of Canada had reviewed the case and seen no problem. In 1995, the UN Committee Against Torture warned that the Canadian government's proposed expulsion of a Pakistani asylum-seeker to Pakistan would violate the Convention Against Torture, even though the individual had enjoyed access to the applicable appeal procedures in Canada. As a result, in 1996 the country that had championed refugee women's rights at the UN Fourth World Conference on Women, appeared in the Report of the UN Special Rapporteur against Torture. Canada had also expelled a refugee claimant back to Zaire against her express request. Canada argued that she had been allowed the benefit of Canada's appeal procedures. (There are allegations that the refugee claimant woman was drugged illegally by immigration officials to facilitate the expulsion. The matter of illegal drugging is still in litigation.)

That there are problems with its appeal procedures is well known to the Canadian government. Before the latest series of changes in legislation in 1989, the UN High Commissioner for Refugees pointed out that Canada's lack of a mechanism for appeal on a case's merits was likely to pose problems. A government-commissioned report, "The Quality of Mercy," by Susan Davis and Lorne Waldman, was released in April 1994. The document calls for a series of reforms that would provide a simpler but stronger appeal mechanism prior to expulsion: a centralized review of refugee status decisions; independent decision makers to judge "risk" and "humanitarian issues"; clearly defined objective criteria; reasons for decisions; and access to judicial review.

In 1995, a former Deputy Minister of Justice was appointed to report on expulsion proceedings after newspaper revelations appeared stating that immigration officials had forged signatures in order to obtain documents necessary to expel failed refugee claimants. "Removals: Process and People in Transition" by Roger Tasse was released in February 1996. The report is short on criticism and couched in the hope of better things to come, but the recommendations speak for themselves: published statistics on expulsion; a responsive complaint mechanism; and the possibility of review by an independent authority.

There is some good news in Canada's treatment of refugees. The Canadian Human Rights Commission in its annual report found the requirement of fees to obtain permanent resident status (and thereby family reunion) inappropriate. The bad news is that the current Bill C49 will take away the right of refugee claimants to benefit from the best of two decision makers at the Immigration and Refugee Board. Henceforth, only one will be required. Meanwhile, appointments to the Refugee Board are still what a Canadian Bar Association report in 1990 referred to as "patronage appointments."

The United States and Immigration Legislation

In 1994, legislation was introduced in the U.S. Congress to "reform" immigration law. Reflecting the backlash against immigrants and the passage in California of Proposition 187, the legislation imposed draconian cuts in legal immigration (some proposals cutting immigration levels by two-thirds), elimination of benefits for immigrants, strong enforcement measures to beef up border control, and dozens of other initiatives that would make it more difficult for refugees and immigrants to receive services or benefits, or to sponsor family members. In view of this assault, Church World Service and two other church-based refugee agencies—Lutheran Immigration and Refugee Service (LIRS) and Episcopal Migration Ministries (EMM)—launched the Refugee Protection Campaign with the purpose of mobilizing their church-based constituencies to speak out on these issues.

Unlike most church-based advocacy in the United States, this campaign concentrated on a few specific issues and targeted a few key congressional representatives. Although most of the provisions in the legislation were bad, the campaign focused on the three that would have the most negative impact on people in need of protection, and that were of particular concern to churches. First, the legislation would cut the number of refugees admitted to the United States by half. Second, it would eliminate humanitarian parole, a procedure used by the U.S. government to admit people for particular humanitarian reasons—for example, an aging woman who might not qualify as a refugee but who would be unable to survive in her home country with all of her children resettled in the United States. Third, the legislation would enable INS officials to return immediately any asylum-seeker arriving with false documents. While this procedure, known as summary exclusion, was intended to send a message to smugglers and others engaged in fraudulent practices, the fact is that in many oppressive situations, people fearing persecution have no alternative but to use forged documents to get out of the country.

The campaign produced short background sheets focusing on these three issues and began to mobilize churches in those states that had representatives in Congress who were key to passage of the bill. Thousands of churches that had sponsored refugees in the past were urged to contact their members of Congress and tell about their positive experiences. Timely information was provided so that churches could press their representatives at the right moment in the legislative process. Members of one ecumenical group in Los Angeles, for example, generated eight thousand letters and telephone calls to their representative—overnight. A harried congressional staffer called the Church World Service office pleading for a respite. "Our phone lines are all tied up," he said. "Please call off the churches."

The campaign organized a series of refugee lobby days in which individual refugees and asylum-seekers were brought to Washington to meet with congressional representatives and staff to tell their stories. This turned out to be a wonderful experience. When faced with stories of escape and persecution, congressional representatives had a hard time defending the legislative initiatives that would cut refugee admissions.

The legislative process in the United States is long, and the immigration reform bill went through many changes before it was finally adopted in September 1996. But, in the course of the process, the cuts in refugee admissions were eliminated from the legislation, the worst aspects of summary exclusion were taken out, and the measures eliminating humanitarian parole were removed. In other words, the church-based Refugee Protection Campaign succeeded in all three of its priorities. Through this campaign, the church-based agencies realized that they had a tremendous natural constituency that could be mobilized to affect legislative policy. Not only could enough people be mobilized to generate thousands of letters and telephone calls, but individual pastors and lay people had important political connections that they were more than willing to use. A meeting, for example, between a dozen pastors and a senator in his office back home is a significant statement of the churches' concern. By focusing on a few issues and providing guidance about the timing of the response, the campaign moved well beyond the churches' usual practice—asking members to write letters to their congressional representatives on all issues all of the time.

While the Refugee Protection Campaign was a powerful expression of the churches' advocacy role in the United States, the fact remains that the current pervasive anti-immigrant backlash also exists in our churches. There is much hard work to be done in our congregations in the areas of education and the raising of awareness about refugee and immigration issues. There is also increasing concern about the impact of welfare reform on immigrants. Almost half of the savings in welfare reform were achieved by cutting benefits to immigrants. Most vulnerable are the elderly and disabled who face elimination of Supplemental Social Security benefits. Fear of losing such benefits has led to a dramatic increase in the number of applications for U.S. citizenship. However, once again, the elderly (who have often not learned to speak English) and the disabled (some of whom may not be able to swear an oath of allegiance) face particular difficulties in their efforts to become naturalized citizens.

Advocacy

Work with refugees and immigrants in the United States and Canada is becoming more difficult on all levels. With changing demographics, financial pressures, and declining church membership, it is harder and harder to find congregations willing to sponsor refugees or provide volunteers who can assist them in their adjustment to life in North America.

Because of economic pressures, both the United States and Canada are reducing their assistance to refugees in other countries. Since 1994, both nations have cut their financial support of international agencies that work with refugees (see table below). The amount of assistance per capita given by Canada and the United States is substantially less than that of many far smaller developed countries—and it is shrinking.

Contributions to International Refugee Agencies

(including UNHCR, the International Organization for Migration, and the UNRWA, the UN agency working with Palestinian refugees)

Country	Contribution per capita	Contribution in US millions
Norway-1994	$13.53	$58.20
Norway-1995	$14.97	$64.36
Netherlands-1994	$5.10	$78.54
Netherlands-1995	$6.10	$94.61
USA-1994	$1.53	$397.74
USA-1995	$1.46	$383.19
Canada-1994	$1.48	$43.03
Canada-1995	$1.08	$31.84

—From *World Refugee Survey, 1995* and *1996*. Washington, DC: U.S. Committee for Refugees.

The churches need to speak out on these issues. Many decisions that are being made for political reasons touch on profoundly moral dilemmas. What is our responsibility to refugees in other parts of the world? What should be the balance between assisting refugees overseas and accepting refugees for resettlement? In a world of limited resources, which groups of people should have access to U.S. and Canadian resettlement programs?

What responsibility does society have toward its members, particularly the most vulnerable? How do we balance the need of immigrants to cherish their own cultures with the needs of the nation-state? These questions underlie many political decisions now being made.

In a climate that has made it politically popular to blame immigrants for social and political problems, and at a time in which politicians do not take immigrants seriously as a constituency, it is particularly important that churches speak up on behalf of immigrants and refugees. Congregations have been involved with them for many years and can speak from experience about the contributions that refugees bring. Politicians often hear about the problems; they also need to hear about the countless refugees who become productive members of society.

Beyond the statistics and the headlines are individual human beings—with their stories of terror and hope, of triumphs and disappointments. When all is said and done, perhaps the most important contribution that the churches can make to the policy debate is to keep a clear focus on individual human beings, to enable refugees and immigrants to tell their own stories. It may be the best way of raising awareness and educating the public—including the church's membership!—about the issues affecting refugees and immigrants. Many people outside the church are deeply concerned, as well, but the church has always had a special mandate to speak out for the most vulnerable in our society. We, who comprise the church, dare not neglect that responsibility.

FIVE

Becoming
the Church of the Stranger

On the road to Emmaus, two disciples run into a stranger and strike up a conversation about recent events in Jerusalem. When they invite him home for dinner (how many of us would do that?) they discover that the stranger in their midst is Jesus Christ. It is within the context of their hospitality—the sharing of a meal with his followers—that Christ reveals himself and the glorious story of the resurrection. We are reminded of Hebrews 13:2, where we are urged to welcome strangers because by so doing we may, unknowingly, have entertained angels. One theme of the gospel message is to open ourselves to the power of stories told by strangers, because God may be speaking through them.

Another theme is that by ministering to strangers and to the uprooted, we minister to Jesus Christ. The powerful story of the Last Judgment in Matthew 25 tells us that when we serve the stranger, feed the hungry, clothe the naked, or visit the prisoner we are serving our Lord. Christ not only calls on us to serve the stranger, but he identifies with the stranger. He tells us that he *is* the stranger.

In September 1995, the governing body of the World Council of Churches adopted a statement on the uprooted, challenging churches around the world to express their solidarity with uprooted people in their communities. The statement includes a long list of actions that local congregations can take, depending on their particular social and political contexts: they might, for example, invite a refugee or an immigrant to join them for a meal, or they could advocate more humane policies by their governments toward immigrants arriving on their borders. But even more profound than all these actions is the reality of churches and individual Christians opening themselves to the experiences of the stranger—to move beyond hearing stories and *become* the church of the stranger.

We are all strangers on some level. In a very literal sense, most of us have had the experience of moving to new neighborhoods. Probably each of us has at some time been an outsider. But in a larger sense, we are all exiles because of our identity as Christians. When we try to live by gospel values in our secular societies, we are reminded again and again that we are not of this world. To become the church of the stranger is to acknowledge our common uprootedness.

Starting with a Story

Work with the uprooted is always personal. You begin with the story of an individual—a person forced to leave his or her home. Getting to the heart of the story is a bit like peeling off the layers of an onion. You start to ask questions, and as you discover what that individual endured, the questions multiply.

"How did you get out of Somalia?" I asked the woman sitting in my office in Geneva. She told a harrowing story of travel by night through the desert, of being robbed and abandoned by a smuggler, of drinking camel urine, of finally arriving at the border where she was raped by border guards before she stumbled into town to find a relative. It was a terrible story. But it was also a story of strength and perseverance—she was a survivor. She had made it through the desert that night and eventually made it to Canada. Hearing that story led to other questions: Why did you have to leave Somalia? Why can't you go back? How are you faring in Canada? Would I have been that strong in her situation?

—From the author's account of her interview with a refugee from Somalia, n.d.

Each question leads to other questions, other complexities, other stories. They are stories we need to hear. It is in listening and trying to understand that we learn about individual refugees and the complex social, economic, and political forces that uproot people. As we "peel the onion," as we open ourselves to the stories, we also learn about ourselves. And if we take seriously the words of the gospel, we may hear messages from God in the refugees' stories. "Do not neglect to show hospitality to strangers, for by doing that some have entertained angels without knowing it." Obviously, not all refugees are angels or messengers from God, but by opening ourselves to the stories of individuals forced to flee their communities, we may find that we ourselves are changed.

To respond to the gospel mandate, we must reach out to the strangers in our communities. Taking that first step of smiling at strangers, of learning where they come from and why they have come to our community is often the most difficult step. In order to really hear the stories, we need to overcome our fears and prejudices. We must also remember, however, that although individual stories are often compelling, the larger national and international issues swirling around immigration are often deeply complicated and defy easy answers.

Why do I become uneasy when we start talking about strangers in my community? It's easy enough to talk about helping them "over there." Why do they have to come here—they can't all come here anyway. Don't I have a right to feel comfortable in my own church? Do we really want to be a multicultural society?

Underlying the resistance to foreigners and opposition to immigration is fear—not just of people and cultures that are unfamiliar to us, but also fear of the impact on our communities and way of life. Sometimes this is the result of stereotypes we hold, consciously or unconsciously, in our own minds. It is relatively clear that people should not be forced to leave their homes.

However, if they are uprooted, are other countries morally or legally bound to take them in? When people move to another country do they have to give up their culture? What is the balance between helping poor people who are long-term citizens of our country and extending a welcome to strangers? Shouldn't we take care of our own first? Particularly for those of us living in rich countries, there are legitimate concerns about the impact of immigrants on the environment and responsible use of the world's resources. We know, for example, that a person living in North America uses far more natural resources than someone living in Africa or Latin America. If more people come to North America, will that mean less for those who have lived in Canada or the United States for generations? Do we—many of us with ancestors who were allowed to settle in this land—have a right to slam the door on those who seek to come now?

The issues are complex. Like the onion, there are layers upon layers of questions. Grappling with the issues and listening to individual stories constitute a first step toward action.

Taking the First Step

Around the world, churches have been in the forefront of ministry to the uprooted. As noted in the first chapter of this book, since biblical times they have welcomed the persecuted, fed the hungry, and provided shelter to the foreigner. In today's world, where unprecedented numbers of people are being uprooted by violence and starvation, the forms of Christian witness and service reflect the different cultures in which Christians live and work. When we begin to wonder what we can do with and for the uprooted, we are in good company.

In the mid-1980s, the West German government became alarmed at the increase in people who asked for political asylum at its airports. In an effort to reduce their numbers, and to ensure that these individuals did not enter the country to begin the official process of seeking asylum, the government set up strict new procedures—in the airports. An individual asking for asylum at the immigration counter was no longer taken to a reception center in town and given months to prepare his or her application. Rather, that person was held at the airport while undergoing preliminary interviews that would determine a ruling on his or her claim. In effect, for several years West Germany's airports were filled with asylum-seekers waiting for someone to tell them whether they could enter the country to tell their story. In Frankfurt's bustling airport, for example, tired women washed their babies in airport restrooms; outside the restroom doors glittered duty-free shops advertising gold watches and expensive cognac. These asylum-seekers were invisible to most Germans; they were not let out of the airport.

In a remarkable effort to respond to the needs of these people, the German churches negotiated with the authorities and began an airport ministry. Individual Christians and church agencies provided meals and coffee, clean clothes, and company for the asylum-seekers. They also offered a measure of protection, since they met airplanes at the same time as the border ministry officials and witnessed what was said and done.

Since then, the German government, like other governments in Europe and North America, has developed more sophisticated means to prevent asylum-seekers from arriving in its airports. Now, visas are required for people traveling from countries in which there is widespread violence. A person trying to escape persecution in Sri Lanka or Iraq, for example, must now get a visa before being allowed to board an airplane. It is clearly difficult for someone persecuted by his or her government to apply for a passport from that government or to convince an embassy consular officer that he or she is planning to return. But today German airport authorities no longer have to worry about hundreds of asylum-seekers sleeping in the transit lounges. And the German churches are concentrating their efforts on serving asylum-seekers who are allowed into the country, as well as on changing their government's policy.

In the early 1980s, as war raged in the Central American countries of Guatemala and El Salvador, hundreds of thousands of Central Americans made their way to the United States. However, the Central Americans were not welcomed by the U.S. government. Even as the United States was granting massive amounts of military aid to the Salvadoran government, hundreds of thousands of Salvadorans were turning up on U.S. borders. President Ronald Reagan used fear of the refugees to buttress his policies in the region, referring to a "tidal wave" of refugees swarming into our country "if the leftist movements in Central America were successful." To recognize the Central Americans as refugees would have been to acknowledge the violence in their home countries and to recognize that the governments which the United States was supporting were not protecting their own citizens.

The U.S. government's rates of approval for Central American asylum-seekers were very low. In 1984, for example, only three of 761 Guatemalan applicants (less than 0.5 percent) and 328 of 13,373 Salvadorans (less than 2.5 percent) were granted asylum. During the same period, approval rates for Russians and Bulgarians were 51 and 52 percent, respectively. Many Central Americans were apprehended, detained, and subsequently deported. Estimates of the number of Salvadorans deported by the Immigration and Naturalization Service ranged from five hundred to one thousand per month. Many more Salvadoran and Guatemalan refugees lived in constant fear that they would be sent back.

In this context, a number of U.S. churches declared themselves public sanctuaries for refugees who were not recognized as such by the government. In so doing, they invoked the Old Testament tradition of cities of refuge for those fleeing persecution. By the mid-1980s, some four hundred congregations and other community groups had offered sanctuary to Central American refugees in direct defiance of U.S. policy. In Canada, churches and nongovernmental organizations formed Vigil, a group that monitored the fate of Central Americans who were rejected as refugees by the Canadian authorities. The sanctuary movement was a grassroots response by United States churches at a particular moment in time, but its impact extended far beyond U.S. borders. Churches in the Netherlands, Sweden, and the United Kingdom declared their congregations sanctuaries for asylum-seekers whose appeals for refugee status had been rejected by their governments.

In Malawi—a country that for a decade was host to more than a million Mozambican refugees—international church agencies mounted major programs to serve people living in camps. For years, though on a smaller scale, members of individual Malawian congregations visited the refugees, organized church services, and helped widows build homes. The Mozambican refugees eventually departed, grateful that the long war was over and that they could begin to rebuild their lives. Churches in poor countries often seem far more willing to share what they have than do those in more affluent regions.

In York County, Pennsylvania, a Methodist minister, Joan Maruskin, learned that the Chinese immigrant men whose ship, the *Golden Venture*, had gone aground in New York, were now detained in the York County detention center. She had not been involved with refugees or immigrants before—had never really thought about immigration issues. But on the day that she learned of the Chinese detained in her county, the lectionary reading was from Exodus 3: "I have heard the cries of my people. . . . I have come to bring them to a good and broad land. . . . I will send you to Pharaoh to bring my people out of Egypt. . . . I will be with you." Pastor Maruskin reports that she felt God was speaking directly to her; she was overcome with a powerful sense that she had to learn more about these strangers who had suddenly been dropped into York County, Pennsylvania. She visited the detention center and tried to communicate with the Chinese men. Then she talked about her visits with other Christians in her community. Eventually, an interfaith coalition calling itself "People of the Golden Vision" was established "in response to God's words and a belief in justice and the interconnectedness of all people, [working] to develop public support for and to assure compassionate and just treatment of all persons fleeing persecution and seeking asylum within the borders of the United States."

The interfaith group brought together an unusual assortment of concerned individuals, including anti-abortion activists who were angered by the treatment of people fleeing their government's forced abortion policies. Members of the group met and prayed together, trying to discern God's will for their ministry. They adopted individual Chinese as pen pals—committing themselves to visit and write to one of the detainees every week. (This was a particular challenge, as the Chinese spoke no English—and none of the Americans spoke Chinese.) Each Sunday evening they held a service of Exodus, Freedom, and Justice near the prison, in sight of the men from the *Golden Venture.* The group examined the legal status of the men and concluded that they were getting short shrift on their asylum claims; that the procedures being used to deny their claims were unfair. So, they mobilized a network of attorneys willing to donate their time to provide legal counsel to the asylum-seekers. The group also set up a network of congregations that agreed to receive and care for any Chinese detainees who were released from detention. They mobilized medical care and support for those who were released.

The story of these Chinese men is almost over. Many were deported, some choosing to return, in part, because of their experiences here in prison. Others remained for more than three years. In February 1997, as a direct result of the work of the interfaith coalition, President Clinton agreed to release the Chinese pending their asylum claims. The People of the Golden Vision organized a final worship service and arranged homes and jobs for all the men who were released. For the People of the Golden Vision it was a powerful, compelling witness and service, directly motivated by the words of the Bible. Their lives have been changed and they have expanded their work to support other refugees and immigrants who are out of the public eye in detention centers around the country.

A world away, in Cairo, Egypt, a small Anglican church served English-speaking expatriates for years. Attracting diplomats and business people, St. Andrew's sought to minister to the needs of the country's small English-speaking expatriate community. But as the war in southern Sudan intensified, the number of Sudanese coming to Egypt increased. By the mid-1990s, an estimated 2 million Sudanese were living in Egypt—some fleeing the bloody war in the south, others in search of economic opportunities. Many of them were Christians and came to St. Andrew's. In a remarkably short time, comfortable Anglican expatriate St. Andrew's had grown and changed until 90 percent of its membership consisted of Sudanese refugees.

The congregation's attitudes, perceptions, and interests broadened and changed. Now, in the middle of a coffee hour after Sunday morning services, the parishioners stop for a few moments of silent prayer for peace in Sudan and throughout the world. The church developed new ministries of outreach to the Sudanese, providing English classes, clothing, food, and company for the strangers who turned up on their doorstep. The war in southern Sudan continues, and the Sudanese continue to live as uprooted people in Cairo. By welcoming the Sudanese, the people of St. Andrew's sought to respond to the strangers who arrived at their doors. In the process, the congregation was transformed.

In most countries throughout the world, there is risk involved in working with the uprooted. In some it may mean death, imprisonment, or persecution. In others, it is the risk of taking politically unpopular views or of daring to reach out to those whom many see as unworthy. Currently in North America, speaking out on behalf of immigrants and refugees goes against the tide of public opinion. It is not always comfortable to be praying in a field across from a detention center or to go looking for immigrants in our communities. But when we take this kind of action, we do so in solidarity with church partners elsewhere in the world for whom work with the uprooted is personally dangerous. In Sri Lanka, the national YMCA is engaged in work of peace and reconciliation with young people from different ethnic groups. The YMCA could choose to concentrate on recreation for middle class children instead of developing programs to serve the displaced and to help bring about an end to the terrible violence in that country.

Churches struggling in different parts of the world to express solidarity with uprooted people often feel isolated and powerless. Recognition that they are not alone in these struggles is a powerful antidote to burnout. On a global level, the World Council of Churches has encouraged ecumenical bodies to form regional working groups focusing on uprooted people. In North America, ecumenical groups meet two or three times a year to share information about current developments in Canada, the United States, and Mexico. Once a year, representatives from all of the regions come together under the auspices of the World Council of Churches to compare notes and develop common strategies. Known as the Global Ecumenical Network on Uprooted People, this annual conference provides the participants with an important forum for discerning global trends and working out coordinated ecumenical responses. While the issues and contexts vary, the shared commitment to the gospel message and the recognition that we are all facing difficult times is a source of hope and inspiration.

Addressing the Causes

Responding to the strangers among us—and to the needs of the uprooted in places far from our own communities—is part of what it means to become the church of the stranger. There are many ways to move in this direction, including the following: refusing to laugh at ethnic jokes and challenging the tellers of such jokes; inviting an immigrant to speak to a church group; organizing a school program celebrating cultural diversity; tutoring a refugee in English; advocating continued support of countries struggling to implement a fragile peace. But perhaps the most challenging part of the churches' ministry with the uprooted is addressing the causes that drive people out of their homes in the first place.

> No film can adequately depict the suffering, the fear, and the terror that my people are experiencing. Sarajevo is awash in blood and graves are appearing everywhere. I beg you in the name of the Bosnian children never to allow this to happen to you or to people anywhere else.
> —Edina, age 12, from former Yugoslavia. From *The State of the World's Children, 1996*, p. 15. Geneva: United Nations Children's Fund (UNICEF), 1996.

Sometimes the issues seem so enormous, the hatreds so intense, the politics so complex that it is hard to see what one small local group can do. What about Rwanda, for example? We don't need to know all the answers or even understand what all the issues are. A first step could be to tell our lawmakers that we care about these countries, that we want to support efforts to bring about an end to the suffering of their people. Lawmakers hear from their constituents most frequently about issues on the domestic public agenda. But there are many other things that receive little media coverage or public attention. We need to speak out on those matters as well—and give our support to groups that are working on answers. The churches have a powerful collective voice that needs to be heard. Working with uprooted people can be a transforming experience for individuals and congregations. Over and over again, congregations and individual Christians report that they intended to help refugees or immigrants in their communities, but in the process of trying to help *them*, discovered that they *received* far more than they gave.

> The staff of the Interfaith Refugee Ministry, the Church World Service affiliate in New Haven, Connecticut, fostered an interreligious coalition of nine churches and a synagogue in the commu-

nities of Waterford, East Lyme, and Old Lyme to act as sponsors for Rwandan refugees who had fled genocide in their home country. The Mwizerwa and Uwonkunda families were marched from their homes at gunpoint when civil war broke out. "When they were taken from their home, they had a Bible and a radio," recounts the Reverend Steven Hulme of St. John's Episcopal Church, which is part of the Interfaith Refugee Committee which helped resettle the families. "After twenty years of welcoming refugees from around the world, getting to know these families was different for us. When I first met Mr. Japhet Mwizerwa, he asked, 'Are you a pastor? . . . an Anglican?' I said 'Yes' and he said 'We are too!' We don't have a lot of African Americans in our congregation, and suddenly we have twelve. The church is really enjoying getting to know these lovely families. The refugee ministry is the most significant ecumenical or interfaith project our church has had by far."

Many churches and individuals around the world are responding to uprooted people within their own contexts. The forms those ministries take are as varied as the people themselves. For churches in Thailand it may mean supporting efforts to feed Burmese refugees on their border. For Lebanese churches, responding to the needs of the uprooted means working with refugees from foreign countries as well as internally displaced Lebanese struggling to find their place after sixteen long years of war.

For churches in the United States and Canada, reaching out to the strangers in our midst or advocating with increasingly hostile governments is not easy. Furthermore, our lives are often so full with earning a living, maintaining a family—sometimes mere survival—that there seems to be no time to support yet another good cause. Nevertheless, if we are faithful to the gospel—to welcome the stranger and work for justice—we have no choice. It must be our task and responsibility to open our eyes to the uprooted among us and be there for them. Let us take to heart the words in the book of Hebrews that it is our privilege and duty as Christians to welcome strangers, for by doing so we may unknowingly have entertained angels in our midst.

Appendix

Host Countries and the Numbers of Refugees and Asylum-Seekers They Were Harboring, 31 December 1996

Africa **3,684,000**

Algeria	114,000	Liberia	100,000
Angola	9,300	Libya	27,200
Benin	11,000	Mali	15,000
Burkina Faso	26,000	Mauritania	15,000
Burundi	12,000	Namibia	1,000
Cameroon	1,000	Niger	27,000
Central Af. Republic	36,400	Nigeria	8,000
Chad	100	Rwanda	20,000
Cote d'Ivoire	320,000	Senegal	51,000
Djibouti	22,000	Sierra Leone	15,000
Egypt	46,000	South Africa	22,500
Eritrea	1,000	Sudan	395,000
Ethiopia	328,000	Tanzania	335,000
Gabon	1,000	Togo	10,000
Gambia	5,000	Tunisia	300
Ghana	35,000	Uganda	225,000
Guinea	650,000	Zaire	455,000
Guinea-Bissau	15,000	Zambia	126,000
Kenya	186,000	Zimbabwe	1,000

The Americas and the Caribbean **233,000**

Argentina	400	Ecuador	200
Belize	8,700	El Salvador	150
Bolivia	550	Guatemala	1,200
Brazil	2,200	Mexico	34,450
Canada	26,100	Nicaragua	900
Chile	200	Panama	650
Colombia	200	Peru	300
Costa Rica	23,150	United States	129,600
Cuba	1,650	Venezuela	1,600
Dominican Republic	600		

East Asia and the Pacific 450,000

Australia	7,400	Papua New Guinea	10,000
China	294,100	Philippines	50
Hong Kong	1,300	Solomon Islands	1,000
Japan	300	Thailand	95,850
Malaysia	5,200	Vietnam	34,400

Europe 2,479,000

Armenia	150,000	Macedonia	5,100
Austria	80,000	Netherlands	46,200
Azerbaijan	249,150	Norway	12,700
Belarus	10,800	Poland	3,200
Belgium	18,200	Portugal	200
Bulgaria	550	Romania	600
Croatia	167,000	Russian Federation	484,000
Cyprus	100	Slovak Republic	2,000
Czech Rep.	2,900	Slovenia	10,300
Denmark	24,600	Spain	7,200
Finland	1,700	Sweden	60,500
France	29,200	Switzerland	41,700
Germany	436,400	Turkey	13,000
Greece	5,600	Ukraine	8,000
Hungary	5,400	United Kingdom	40,500
Ireland	1,800	Yugoslavia	550,000
Italy	10,600		

Middle East 5,841,000

Gaza Strip	716,900	Saudi Arabia	257,850
Iran	2,020,000	Syria	384,400
Iraq	114,400	United Arab Emirates	400
Jordan	1,362,500	West Bank	532,400
Kuwait	42,000	Yemen	54,600
Lebanon	355,100		

South and Central Asia 1,795,000

Afghanistan	18,900	Nepal	109,800
Bangladesh	40,000	Pakistan	1,215,700
India	352,200	Tajikistan	2,200
Kazakhstan	14,000	Turkmenistan	22,000
Kyrgyzstan	17,000	Uzbekistan	3,000

TOTAL 15,337,000

This includes refugees and asylum-seekers who need international protection and/or assistance. The table does not include refugees permanently settled in other countries. Figures for Australia, Canada, U.S. and Europe are, for the most part, for those persons who applied for asylum in 1996.

Source: U.S. Committee for Refugees, <u>World Refugee Survey</u> (Washington: USCR) 1997, pp. 4–5.

Populations in Refugee-Like Situations, 31 December 1995

Host country	Origin	Number
Jordan	Palestinians	800,000
Russian Federation	Former USSR	650,000
Thailand	Burma	350,000
Bangladesh	Pakistan	238,000
Saudia Arabia	Somalia	150,000
Syria	Stateless Kurds	142,000
Kuwait	Kuwait (Bidoon)	127,000
Tanzania	Burundi	100,000
Syria	Palestinians	64,000
Mexico	Guatemala	50-100,000
Jordan	Iraq	50,000
Uzbekistan	Tajikistan	30,000
Belize	Central America	28,500
Kyrgyzstan	Tajikistan	30,000
Belarus	Former USSR	24,000
Lebanon	Palestinians	22,000
Nepal	Bhutan	18,000
Thailand	Laos	10,000
Southeast Asia	Vietnam	8,292
Uzbekistan	Afghanistan	8,000
Iraq	Kuwait (Bidoon)	6,000
Iraq	Iran	3,000
Lithuania	Various	3,000
Pakistan	Somalia	1,000

This includes people who may fear persecution but who are not recognized by governments as refugees or asylum-seekers. Some are given temporary refuge or allowed to remain on humanitarian grounds. Others are undocumented. Estimates of their numbers vary widely.

Source: U.S. Committee for Refugees, <u>World Refugee Survey</u> (Washington: USCR), 1997, p. 11.

Countries with Large Numbers of Internally Displaced Persons, 31 December 1995

Sudan 4,000,000
Afghanistan 1,200,000
Angola 1,200,000
Bosnia and Hercegovina 1,000,000
Liberia 900,000
Sri Lanka 900,000
Sierra Leone 800,000
Colombia 600,000
Azerbaijan 550,000
Turkey 500,000-2,000,000
Burma 500,000-1,000,000
South Africa 500,000
Lebanon 450,000
Peru 420,000
Burundi 400,000
Russian Federation 400,000
Zaire 400,000
Georgia 285,000
Cyprus 265,000
India 250,000
Somalia 250,000
Guatemala 200,000
Croatia 185,000
Syria 125,000
Kenya 100,000
Papua New Guinea 70,000
Uganda 70,000
Armenia 50,000
Tajikistan 50,000
Cambodia 32,000
Nigeria 30,000
Djibouti 25,000
Ghana 20,000
Algeria 10,000

Source: U.S. Committee for Refugees, <u>World Refugee Survey</u> (Washington: USCR), 1997, p. 8.

Notes

Chapter Two

1 Hal Kane, *The Hour of Departure: Forces that Create Refugees and Migrants,* (Washington, DC: Worldwatch Institute), p. 39.

2 *Christian Faith and the World Economy Today: A Study Document from the World Council of Churches,* (Geneva: World Council of Churches, 1992), p. 18.

3 Shawn Roberts and Jody Williams, *After the Guns Fall Silent: The Enduring Legacy of Landmines,* (Washington, DC: Vietnam Veterans of America, 1995).

4 Ibid., p. 19.

5 Susan George, *The Debt Boomerang,* (London: Zed Books, 1992), p. 163.

Chapter Four

1 Guy Vassall-Adams, *Rwanda: An Agenda for International Action,* (Oxford: Oxfam, 1994), p. 12.

2 *The State of the World's Refugees,* 1996, (Geneva: UNHCR), p. 166.

For Further Reading

World Refugee Survey. This definitive resource presents the most comprehensive statistical data available on uprooted people, as well as articles discussing global trends and reports about every country in the world. May be ordered from U.S. Committee for Refugees, 1717 Massachusetts Ave. NW, Suite 701, Washington, DC 20036.

Bau, Ignatius. *This Ground Is Holy.* New York: Paulist Press, 1985.

Building Hospitable Communities, Resource Packet. May be ordered from the Ecumenical Networks Office, National Council of the Churches of Christ in the USA, 475 Riverside Drive, New York, NY 10115.

Changing Relations: Newcomers and Established Residents in U.S. Communities. New York: The Ford Foundation, 1993.

Deng, Francis. *Protecting the Dispossessed: A Challenge for the International Community.* Washington, DC: Brookings Institute, 1993.

Ferris, Elizabeth G. *Beyond Borders: Refugees, Immigrants and Human Rights in the Post-Cold War Era.* Geneva: World Council of Churches, 1993.

Golden, Renny, and Michael McConnell. *Sanctuary: The New Underground Railroad.* New York: Orbis Books, 1986.

Goodwin-Gill, Guy. *The Refugee in International Law*, 2nd ed. Oxford: Oxford University Press, 1997.

Loescher, Gil. *Beyond Charity: International Cooperation and the Global Refugee Crisis.* New York: Oxford University Press, 1993.

Loescher, Gil, and John Scanlan. *Calculated Kindness: Refugees and America's Half-Open Door.* New York: Free Press, 1986.

McCullum, Hugh. *The Angels Have Left Us: The Rwanda Tragedy and the Churches.* Geneva: World Council of Churches, 1995.

A Moment to Choose: Risking to Be with Uprooted People, A Resource Book. Geneva: World Council of Churches, 1997.

Quiroz, Julia Teresa. *Together in Our Differences: How Newcomers and Established Residents Are Rebuilding America's Communities.* Washington, DC: National Immigration Forum, 1995. May be ordered from National Immigration Forum, 220 I Street, NE, Suite 220, Washington, DC 20002.

Roberts, Shawn, and Jody Williams. *After the Guns Fall Silent: The Enduring Legacy of Landmines.* Washington, DC: Vietnam Veterans of America, 1995.

Skeldon, Ronald. *Population Mobility in Developing Countries: A Reinterpretation.* New York: Wiley, 1993.

Teitelbaum, Michael S., and Myron Weiner, eds. *Threatened Peoples, Threatened Borders.* New York: W.W. Norton & Co., 1995.

UNHCR, *The State of the World's Refugees.* Geneva: UNHCR. Issued biannually. May be ordered from UNHCR, 1775 K Street NW, Washington, DC or 280 Albert Street, Suite 401, Ottawa, Ontario K1P 5G8.

Uprooted Peoples: Communities of Hope, Global Education and Advocacy Resource (GEAR). May be ordered from United Church of Christ, 475 Riverside Drive, Suite 1600, New York, NY 10115.

Vassal-Adams, Guy. *Rwanda: An Agenda for International Action,* Oxford: Oxfam, 1994.

Zolberg, Aristedeh, Astri Suhrke, and Sergio Aguayo. *Escape from Violence: Globalized Social Conflict and the Refugee Crisis in the Developing World.* New York: Oxford University Press, 1989.

Especially for Children:

Worldwind: Mission Magazine for Children. Special issue, "Refugees." Order from The United Church of Canada, 3250 Bloor Street, West, Etobicoke, ON (Single copies $2.50; ten or more $2.25.)

Videography
All listed videos are in ½" VHS format.

Primary Resources

No Place to Call Home
Sale: $29.95   Rental: $15.00   1997   26:30

Official estimates now place their number at more than 50 million: women, men, and children who through no fault of their own have been forced to leave their homes and livelihood. Some are victims of civil war, others of persecution or political intimidation. Many are economic refugees who leave in order to survive. This video explores the causes of today's crisis of the uprooted by helping viewers understand what it means to be an uprooted person. It tells compelling human stories, including individual testimonies, of tremendous courage in the face of almost overwhelming odds, and it bears witness to models of compassionate sharing. The video concentrates on Rwanda, Bosnia, and Guatemala. It will move you to anger, perhaps to tears—possibly to action. Study guide included.

Available for *sale only* from Friendship Press Distribution Office, P.O. Box 37844, Cincinnati, OH 45222 0844; Tel. (513) 948 8733. Available for *rental only* from EcuFILM, 810 Twelfth Avenue, South, Nashville, TN 37203; Tel. (800) 251-4091 or (615) 242-6277.

Make a Little Difference
Sale: $19.95   Rental: $15.00   1991   13:00

Produced by UNHCR (United Nations High Commissioner for Refugees), this is an excellent resource for introducing children to the reality of refugees. Faces and voices of children are heard and shown—13-year-olds from Ethiopia and Uganda as refugees in Kenya; a 12-year-old Vietnamese refugee from Thailand. Although they live in extremely difficult situations, positive images are shown. Also included: illustrated *Declaration of the Rights of the Child*. The video is most effective for those 10 years old or older; also an effective intergenerational piece. Study guide included.

Available for *sale only* from Friendship Press Distribution Office [see above]. Available for *rental only* from EcuFILM [see above].

Secondary Resources

Coming Home

Sale: $19.95   Rental: $15.00   1996   15:40

Rwanda has been one of the key "hot spots" of recent years. Fighting between rival tribes of Hutus and Tutsis has led to a flood of refugees. This video shows the work of Christian Aid in Rwanda with fleeing Hutus. Rwanda is suffering a bloodbath, but a new government seeks reconciliation. Also shown is the work of a new organization, ACT (Action by Churches Together). There is a profound need for justice, but at the refugee camps there are simply people in need.

Available for *sale only* from Berkeley Studio, United Church of Canada, 3250 Bloor Street, West, Etobicoke, ON M8X 2Y4, Canada; Tel. (416) 231-5931. Available for *rental only* from EcuFILM [see above].

Companions in Hope

Sale: $24.95   Rental: $15.00   1993   29:00

This video shows the human face of Guatemalan refugees as they return from a refugee camp to their homes. Though they fled as political refugees during the violence of the 80s (primarily to Mexico), they do not want to "take over" so much as simply go home. The camera follows Project Accompaniment from Canada as it goes with the first group of refugees who returned on January 20, 1993.

Available for *sale only* from Berkeley Studio [see above]. Available for *rental only* from EcuFILM [see above].

The Energy of a Nation: Immigrants in America

Sale: $25.00 video only $35.00 with 100-page curriculum guide
1995   11:30

This video is geared toward middle school and high school youth. It provides basic and accurate information about immigration to the United States. Who comes to the United States? How many? Why? What is the impact of immigration on the U.S. economy, labor market, and culture. The video and its accompanying curriculum guide address the economic impact of immigration, its history, current trends, legal and illegal immigration, and government policies. Five immigrants from Vietnam, Iran, South Africa, South Wales, and Spain, respectively, are followed on their journey to Minnesota.

Available for *sale only* from Minnesota Advocates for Human Rights, 400 Second Ave., South, Suite 1050, Minneapolis, MN 55401-2408; Tel. (612) 341-3302.

Lost at Home

Sale: $19.95   Rental: $15.00   1994   18:00

This video is set in Sri Lanka, where there are many purported human rights violations. Churches are concerned about being stopped from working there if they speak out. Women and children are the primary sufferers as the fighting continues, and it is not safe for refugees to return home. The video shows what the people of Sri Lanka are doing for refugees, depicting the positive as well as the negative; and it highlights the work of the church and of church people.

Available for *sale only* from Berkeley Studio [see above]. Available for *rental only* from EcuFILM [see above].

Not the Same Anymore

Sale: $19.95   Rental: $15.00   1992   18:00

This video offers a look at Bosnia and its war-related conflicts. People have been uprooted, and some of the results include sexual violence, loss of honor, and rape as a weapon. In one segment a Somalian women is ostracized because of sexual attacks upon her. The video shows the World Council of Churches working group on refugees and gives many details about what is happening. It is a story that needs to be told.

Available for *sale only* from Berkeley Studio [see above]. Available for *rental only* from EcuFILM [see above].

Strangers in Town

Sale: $19.98 + 3.95 S&H   1993   28:00

Immigrants from Ukraine, Russia, Cambodia, Croatia, Zaire, and Brazil are shown settled into the Boston area. How does their presence affect others already there? This video depicts the use of English as a common language that can empower students, and it demonstrates the effectiveness of programs such as computer training. A disagreement develops with the Haitian community, toward which there is some resentment and resistance but also much positive response. The role of the religious community is emphasized.

Available for *sale only* from CBS-TV; Tel. (800) 494-6007.

The Ties That Bind

Sale: $19.95 +3.00 S&H   1996   56:00

The human drama behind the current debate over U.S. immigration policy is portrayed in this documentary, which is available in both English and Spanish. There are three 20-minute segments: (1) *Good Neighbors and Tall Fences* explores root causes of immigration and the divisive impact of transnational corporations on Latin American immigrants and people in the United States; (2) *Just Between Us* recounts the arduous passage endured by many immigrants, as well as political motivations behind immigration policies; (3) *The Common Bond* shows how today's immigrants continue the tradition of past groups by strengthening the country through their own values of family, faith, and work. Study guide.

Available for *sale only* from Maryknoll World Productions, P.O. Box 308, Maryknoll, NY 10545-0308; Tel. (800) 227-8523.

A Time for Caring

Sale: $19.98 + 3.95 S&H   1996   28:00

Refugees from various of countries settle into the Portland, OR, area, with the help of SOAR (Sponsors Organized to Assist Refugees), an affiliate of Church World Service of the National Council of the Churches of Christ in the USA. The video shows these immigrants in their new communities, and demonstrates the contribution that people from many nations make to the life and culture of the United States. Immigrants from Ukraine, Bosnia, Russia, Somalia, and Laos are assisted by, among others, representatives of United Methodist, Christian, Presbyterian, Southern Baptist, and Roman Catholic churches.

Available for *sale only* from CBS-TV; Tel. (800) 494-6007.

UNHCR: A Global View

Sale: $19.95   Rental: $10.00   1995   20:00

This video provides an overview and the history of UNHCR (United Nations High Commissioner for Refugees), an organization that assists millions of refugees throughout the world each year. One of every 15 people on earth is in flight. There are examples of refugees from Tanzania and Rwanda, as well as an interview with the UN High Commissioner. The video offers an excellent historical perspective and focuses on a variety of important refugee-related concerns such as the distribution of foreign aid. It creates a frame of reference for information that people have learned from the news.

Available from EcuFILM [see above].

We Are Guatemalans

Sale: $14.95 + 3.00 S&H   1994   28:00

After 12 years in Mexico, 2,000 Guatemalan refugees begin the journey back to their homeland. In dramatic accounts they recall a 1982 army massacre in the Ixcan jungle. Narrated by E.G. Marshall. Study guide.

Available for *sale only* from Maryknoll World Productions [see above].